Wagons West

Wagons West

BRIGHAM YOUNG
and the First Pioneers

RICHARD E. TURLEY JR. & LAEL LITTKE

DESERET
BOOK

Salt Lake City, Utah

To pioneers of all ages

Library of Congress Cataloging-in-Publication Data

Names: Turley, Richard E., Jr., 1956– author. | Littke, Lael, author.
Title: Wagons west : Brigham Young and the first pioneers / Richard E. Turley Jr. and Lael Littke.
Description: Salt Lake City, Utah : Deseret Book, [2016] | Includes bibliographical references.
Identifiers: LCCN 2016028001 | ISBN 9781629722504 (hardbound : alk. paper)
Subjects: LCSH: Mormon pioneers—History. | Young, Brigham, 1801–1877. | Mormon Church—History—19th century. | The Church of Jesus Christ of Latter-day Saints—History—19th century.
Classification: LCC BX8611 .T87 2016 | DDC 289.309/034—dc23
LC record available at https://lccn.loc.gov/2016028001

Printed in the United States of America   09/2016
LSC Communications, Harrisonburg, VA

10 9 8 7 6 5 4 3 2 1

Contents

Preface

Wagons West: Brigham Young and the First Pioneers is designed for young readers and others who enjoy a simple but dramatic presentation of historical events. It is divided into chapters of a comfortable length for bedtime reading.

The book closely follows historical sources. All quotations, including dialogue, come from original documents, though we have corrected and updated spelling, capitalization, and punctuation to make the stories easier for young readers to understand. We hope readers of this book might later become interested in more serious history works that deal in greater detail with matters too complicated for this volume.

This book owes a great debt to previous writers, especially the pioneers themselves. We have consciously chosen not to include source notes for fear of discouraging young readers, but we have included a selected bibliography of recommended readings at the end of the volume.

We hope readers will enjoy these stories for many generations to come.

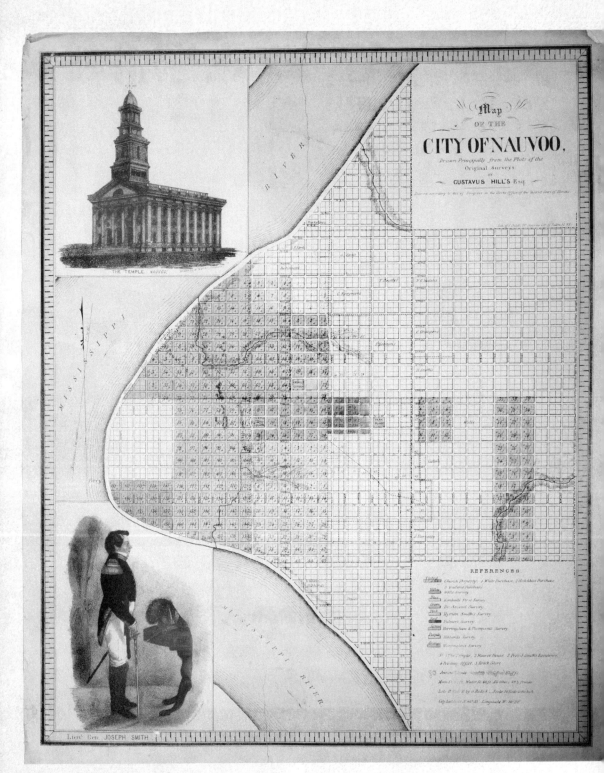

Map of the City of Nauvoo.

Chapter One

Nauvoo the Beautiful

The Saints took pride in their beautiful city of Nauvoo, Illinois, nestled in a bend of the Mississippi River. They had built most of it themselves. So why, in 1845, were mobs demanding that they leave?

Joseph Smith had led a group of people there in 1839 after they were driven out of the state of Missouri. The land that became Nauvoo was mostly a disease-infested swamp then. But Joseph, their president and leader, saw its potential. It would take work, but with heaven's blessing they could turn this land into a gathering place, a place of rest.

These people belonged to The Church of Jesus Christ of Latter-day Saints. They called themselves Saints, but others referred to them as Mormons. This name came from one of their volumes of scripture, the Book of Mormon, which they believed in along with the Bible.

The Saints drained the swampy land and cultivated it. They built new homes and stores and started to erect an imposing temple. They were in the process of setting up a university. They established the Nauvoo Legion, a peace-keeping force authorized by the Illinois state government. It was a stirring sight to see the Legion march through the streets to the music of a brass band.

Nauvoo became a thriving city. Its population soared to around 12,000, almost the same as Chicago, the largest city in Illinois. That worried some non-Mormons. They feared the Mormons wanted to take over the whole state. In fact, the whole country. Hadn't Joseph Smith announced that he planned to run for president of the United States?

That wasn't all. The anti-Mormons said the Mormons were too

Massacre of Saints at Hawn's Mill, Missouri, 1838.

Joseph Smith inspecting the Nauvoo Legion.

close-knit and secretive. Some of them practiced plural marriage. They claimed God required them to do so. They had other strange beliefs. They were different. They had to be stopped. The critics' goal became to get rid of the Mormons.

On June 27, 1844, a swarm of violent men assassinated Joseph Smith and his brother Hyrum. They thought that would stop the Mormons. Elizabeth Ann Smith Whitney wrote later, "The Gentiles, our opposers, thought they had destroyed our religion, overthrown our cause, and destroyed the influence of our people, and actually had accomplished all that was necessary to do away

Carthage Jail, where Joseph and Hyrum Smith were martyred.

with Mormonism. But God's work cannot be ignored; another prophet, Brigham Young, was raised up to succeed Joseph, and the work rolled on."

As time went on, mobs began attacking Latter-day Saint settlements outside Nauvoo. They burned houses and destroyed crops. In the fall of 1845 they set fire to two hundred buildings. Hundreds of people became homeless, and one man was severely beaten.

Sarah Louisa Decker reported, "This is only one of the cruel things that was happening right along on the outskirts of town.

Women and helpless children were carried from a sick bed and laid on the ground while their house and goods were burned. Wheat, haystacks and barns were burned and the cattle driven off."

Brigham Young became the Saints' new leader after Joseph Smith's death. Brigham knew his people had to prepare for the worst. He wrote a letter, instructing them to sell their land and other properties. He told them to gather together "money, wagons, oxen, cows, mules, and a few good horses adapted to journeying and scanty feed."

But where were they to go?

Brigham knew. Even before Joseph Smith's death, Church leaders discussed plans for moving the Saints. Joseph said they must find a place "where we can build a city in a day, and have a government of our own," and "get up into the mountains, where the devil cannot dig us out."

Brigham and the other Church leaders considered many

Brigham Young in the mid-1800s.

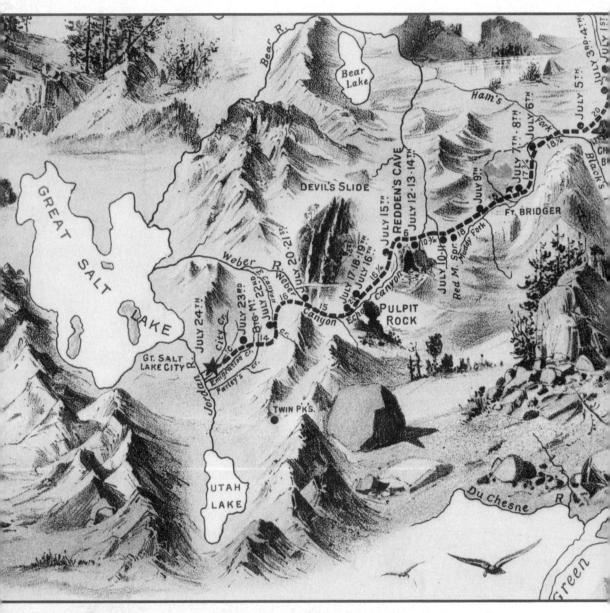

The eastern edge of the Great Basin, where Church leaders planned to move the Saints.

different areas. After much prayer, they decided the Great Basin beyond the Rocky Mountains was the right place to go. They had read reports of fertile land and an abundance of flowing streams. There was also an unusual body of water called the Great Salt Lake. Surrounded by mountains, the Great Basin was a place where the Saints could build a new home and worship as they pleased. Best of all, it was far away from their enemies.

Brigham wanted to follow Joseph's wishes. He urged the people to be of good cheer. He said they should "wake up . . . to the present glorious" situation "in which the God of heaven has placed you." They would find a new home and build another beautiful city, where they could live and worship in peace.

But the place they talked of going was over a thousand miles from Nauvoo. How were they to get there?

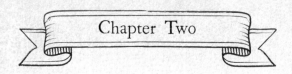

Chapter Two

Driven Out

Brigham Young was a strong man. He was shorter than Joseph Smith, who stood over six feet tall, but like Joseph, he was athletic and energetic. Born in 1801, Brigham had very little formal schooling in his youth. However, he possessed a bright mind and an abundance of common sense. People liked and trusted him.

In 1844, Brigham was the president of the Quorum of the Twelve Apostles. After Joseph died, the Twelve were sustained to lead the Saints. Brigham was president of the quorum but not yet president of the Church. That would come later.

As the violence increased in Nauvoo, Brigham knew the Saints had no choice but to leave. They were being driven out. They had to go, and soon.

But how do you go about moving more than ten thousand people? There were no trains to carry them to find a new home. They would be traveling in wagons or carriages pulled by draft animals, such as oxen or horses. They could take only what would fit into the wagons.

The pioneers fretted. What possessions would they have to leave behind? Would their children be safe? What did their future in the west hold? Despite these worries, they set to work.

Wagons had to be built. Some wagons of the day were big and roomy, but they were also heavy and cumbersome. They weren't suited for a long trek across seemingly endless prairies and high mountains.

Instead the Saints built their smaller, reinforced farm wagons after a St. Louis style of wagon that was about ten feet long. They had to prepare the bed of the wagon for river crossings, using wax to make it water-resistant. And the top of the wagon needed to be covered in canvas, stretched over wooden bows, to protect the contents of the wagon from the elements. The outsides would often be painted bright colors. And the insides

Brigham Young, president of the Quorum of the Twelve Apostles.

Replica of a covered wagon loaded with supplies.

would hold their tools, bedding, and food. The Saints would need a lot of food.

On October 29, 1845, Church leaders published in the *Nauvoo Neighbor* newspaper a list of what the Saints needed to take with them. The list was called a "Bill of Particulars," and it included food and other items that each family needed to travel west. Flour would be a staple, a thousand pounds per family. They would also need rice, beans, dried fruits, bacon or beef, and sugar. A large

BILL OF PARTICULARS

FOR THE EMIGRANTS LEAVING THIS GOVERN-
MENT NEXT SPRING.

Each family consisting of five persons, to be provided with

1 good strong wagon, well covered with a light box.

2 or 3 good yoke of oxen between the age of 4 and 10 years.

2 or more milch cows.

1 or more good beeves.

3 sheep if they can be obtained.

1000 lbs. of flour or other bread or bread stuffs in good sacks.

1 good musket or rifle to each male over the age of 12 years.

1 lb. Powder,

4 do Lead,

25 do Seed grain,

1 gal. Alcohol,

20 lbs of Soap each family,

4 or 5 Fish hooks and lines for do,

15 lbs. Iron and Steel.

A few lbs of wrought nails,

One or more sets of saw or grist mill Irons to company of 100 families,

2 sets of Pully Blocks and ropes to each co'y for crossing rivers,

1 good Seine and hook for each company,

From 25 to 100 lbs. of

A packing list for the Saints as they prepared to leave Nauvoo.

number of seasonings were on the list: salt, pepper, mustard, cinnamon, cloves, and nutmeg.

Families also needed to be prepared to find food along the way. To fish in the rivers, they needed fish hooks and lines. Each family should take two or more cows to provide milk. They would also need seed and farming tools to get started in their new home.

The leaders asked families to gather powder and lead for their guns. They also needed nails, iron, and steel, as well as ropes to help in crossing rivers. In addition, clothes, bedding, furniture,

Some supplies the pioneers took with them.

cooking utensils, and tents had to fit in the wagon. The leaders ended the list with this advice: "Many items of comfort and convenience will suggest themselves to a wise and provident people, . . . but none should start without filling the original bill."

How could they carry all the necessary items in a wagon? How much would it cost? What cherished items would have to be left behind?

Brigham organized the people into twenty-five companies of one hundred, with a captain for each group. The entire city became a beehive of activity. Loads of timber for building the wagons rolled down the streets. Blacksmiths hammered iron into shoes for the horses and oxen. They also fashioned metal rims for the wooden wheels.

But new problems arose. Canvas was needed for the wagon covers, and there was a shortage of that material in Nauvoo. Men traveled to other communities to find more. Then the canvas had to be cut and sewn to fit over the wooden arches of the wagons.

To obtain what they needed for the westward trek, the Saints traded whatever they had. That sometimes included grain and

Oxen were among the animals the pioneers used to pull wagons across the plains.

The completed Nauvoo Temple.

other food supplies that Brigham had previously advised them to gather and store.

When November 1845 ended, 1,508 wagons had been built, with 1,892 more under way. The total of 3,400 wagons would provide one for each family in the twenty-five companies. The remaining 115 wagons could be used for other purposes.

More oxen and horses were needed to pull all these wagons. Oxen were preferred. They were strong, gentle, and patient. They were easier to drive than horses. A widow could transport herself and her children across the plains with a yoke of oxen pulling their wagon.

Brigham hoped his people could stay in Nauvoo through the winter. He made an agreement with the anti-Mormons that if they would stop their persecutions, the Saints would leave when they could. They planned to depart "as early next spring as the first appearance of thrifty vegetation." They needed this vegetation for the animals to feed on along the way.

There was another reason Brigham wanted to remain in Nauvoo until spring. Joseph Smith had felt an urgency to finish the temple. Sacred ceremonies important to the Saints' salvation would be conducted there.

Obedient to what he asked of them, the Saints had made sacrifices to work on the temple. Sarah Louisa Norris Decker wrote, "The temple was being built, and each one seemed to desire to help, and many sold things that they could scarcely spare to put the means towards the building. I can remember of my mother selling her China dishes and fine bed quilt, to donate her part."

After Joseph's death, Brigham and the Twelve felt driven to finish that task too. They figured the temple would be finished by April 1846, and they could dedicate it to the Lord before they left. When it became obvious that they would have to leave before then, however, Brigham urged the Saints to work harder to complete the temple.

Efforts were made to finish the upper rooms where the sacred ceremonies would take place. They plastered and painted the walls. They covered the floors with borrowed carpets. They sewed curtains to hang at the windows. The upper area was dedicated to the Lord on November 30, 1845.

People flocked to the temple to take part in the sacred ceremonies that bound them to their families for eternity. More than five thousand people were able to do so before they had to leave.

But two new threats forced an even earlier departure date than they had planned. One was that Brigham and other Church leaders were unjustly accused of being in partnership with river crooks to run a counterfeiting operation. After Joseph Smith was murdered in Carthage Jail, other Church leaders tried to avoid being arrested for fear of also being killed. They knew they had to leave Nauvoo before other lies brought more trouble.

The other threat was a warning from Governor Ford that federal troops might try to stop the Mormons from heading west.

The Saints' leaders urged people to be ready to go before that happened.

Later the governor admitted he had made up the whole thing. He had hoped the threat would frighten Brigham into evacuating the city immediately. That way the state of Illinois would be rid of the Mormons with no further fuss.

Faced with such animosity from even the governor, Brigham didn't take any chances. In January of 1846 he

Illinois governor Thomas Ford.

asked for reports on the progress of the families in preparing to leave.

What he found out discouraged him. Although hundreds of wagons had been built, only seventy were totally outfitted and ready to go. Since most people thought they couldn't possibly leave before spring, they had not been diligent in getting ready.

Brigham then called a meeting of all company leaders. He wanted to know how many would be "ready and willing to start at a moment's warning, should necessity require it." He spoke of the evil their enemies aimed to do. He had said earlier, "Our danger consists only in being held still by the authorities while mobs massacre us as Governor Ford held Joseph and Hyrum Smith while they were butchered."

Every man at the meeting promised to "do whatever was considered best for the common interest of all."

It was time to start crossing the Mississippi River to Iowa and the wilderness beyond.

Chapter Three

Crossing the Mississippi

Leaving Nauvoo brought up many problems. A big one was crossing the Mississippi River. There were no bridges near Nauvoo. Brigham advised all group captains to locate boats that could ferry oxen and wagons across the river.

He worried about a new report he had received. It said that across the river in Keokuk, Iowa, men disguised in Indian clothing had boasted about how they would capture the Mormon leaders as they crossed the river.

That wasn't all. More rumors circulated that the government was going to interfere, this time by disarming the Saints. The excuse would be that the Mormons were escaping to the territory of another country and needed to be stopped.

The Saints didn't know what to believe. On the one hand, there were people in Illinois who demanded that they get out of Nauvoo. On the other hand, the rumors said there were people who would refuse to let them leave.

These rumors, combined with the uneasy peace in the

surrounding areas, made it clear that the Saints had to leave or be severely persecuted. And they had to do it soon. "Our enemies have resolved to intercept us whenever we start," Brigham said. "I should like to push on as far as possible before they are aware of our movements."

The Saints worried about their property. They needed to sell their homes and farms, but they could not hope to get full value for anything. It seemed as if the entire city was for sale. Buyers could pay as little as they pleased. In a letter to her mother in Massachusetts, Martha Haven wrote, "We have sold our place for a trifle to a Baptist minister. All we got was a cow and two pairs of steers, worth sixty dollars in trade."

Brigham appointed five men to care for and sell all property that could not be disposed of before the Saints left. The owners would have to be satisfied with whatever they could get.

A Missouri River ferry like the ones used by the Saints to cross the Mississippi.

Heber C. Kimball's home in Nauvoo.

Even though it was the dead of winter, the Saints who were ready loaded up their wagons. It was difficult to say good-bye to their warm homes. But they let the flames die down in their fireplaces and left.

Bathsheba Wilson Bigler Smith described it this way: "We left a comfortable home, the accumulations of four years of labor and thrift, and took away with us only a few much-needed articles such as clothing, bedding, and provisions. We left everything else behind us for our enemies. My last act in that precious spot was to tidy the rooms, sweep up the floor, and set the broom in its accustomed place behind the door."

Filled with emotion, Bathsheba closed that door. Although her future was uncertain, she later recalled that she "faced it with faith in God," holding to the "true, enduring principles" of the gospel she loved and sensing "a greater destiny" for her in the West.

After a lingering look back at the almost finished temple, the Saints headed for the Mississippi River, where boats and rafts waited to ferry them over.

The scene at the docks was noise and confusion. Wagons clogged the streets. People shivered in the cold as they waited. Oxen bawled. Frightened children wailed. Mothers attempted to soothe them in the cramped space of the wagons. Men shouted instructions. Drivers tried to follow what they were told as they inched forward.

There was no going back.

George Q. Cannon later said, "Those of us who can remember when we were compelled to abandon Nauvoo, when the winter was so inclement . . . , know how dark and gloomy the circumstances of the Saints were, with the mob surrounding our outer settlements and threatening to destroy us."

"But then," he added, "you can also remember, doubtless, how full of courage and how full of hope the faithful Latter-day Saints were in these trying circumstances. . . . The faith of the Latter-day Saints at that time was unshaken."

On February 4, 1846, the first wagons successfully crossed the river. Many more followed on boats, barges, and skiffs over the next several days. On the other side, they headed for what would be their first campground, at Sugar Creek, Iowa, nine miles away. They would wait there almost two weeks for Brigham, who had stayed in Nauvoo to continue administering temple work, and whoever else was ready to join them.

But the crossing was not easy. The river was deep and almost a mile wide. With so many people and animals, there were bound to be accidents. One occurred when an overloaded skiff began to sink. A nearby flatboat hurried to the rescue and picked up all passengers.

In the crowded conditions on one of the boats, a tobacco-chewing man spat out a mouthful of tobacco juice. It splattered

Saints leaving Nauvoo.

Nauvoo from across the Mississippi River.

into the eye of an ox. The startled beast plunged forward into the river, dragging along its teammate and the wagon they were hitched to. The sideboards of the boat were ripped off, and it took on water.

Men struggled to guide the boat back towards Nauvoo. But it sank before it got there. People in the water grabbed onto anything that would float. "Some were on feather beds, sticks of wood, lumber, or anything they could get hold of," reported a witness.

Fortunately, other boats picked up all the people from the icy river. Rescuers pulled the wagon and its soaked baggage from the water, too. Sadly, the two oxen drowned.

That was not the only misfortune of the day. In the

midafternoon someone spotted flames shooting up from the temple roof. Both men and women rushed to start a bucket brigade. They formed long lines to pass buckets of water into the temple and up to the roof. It was determined that an overheated stovepipe in the attic started the fire.

Brigham was still at his home when he saw the blaze. Before leaving to help, he said to his family, "If it is the will of the Lord that the temple be burned, instead of being defiled by the Gentiles, amen to it." After all, it would have to be rented or sold when the Saints left. Perhaps it was better for it to burn.

Through the valiant efforts of the bucket brigade, however, the fire was put out. Brigham arrived, greeted with shouts of

Two years after the Saints left, the Nauvoo Temple caught fire again. This time it was destroyed.

"Hosannah!" from the men on the roof. They were happy they had been able to save the temple. It was still theirs to protect.

That evening a large crowd of Saints who were still in Nauvoo gathered at the temple to celebrate victory over the fire. There was "music and rejoicing" until well after midnight. When they finally left, they felt they had said a fitting farewell to their beautiful building.

With a good many Saints already on the other side of the river, the wagons continued to cross. On February 14, Parley P. Pratt

Crossing the frozen Mississippi River.

floated his wagons and carriages across the Mississippi. The next day, Sunday, February 15, Brigham said good-bye to his home and headed for the ferry with more than a dozen wagons and fifty family members.

Brigham's history recorded, "I crossed the river with my family accompanied by W. Richards and family and George A. Smith. We travelled on four miles, when we came to the bluff. I would not go on until I saw all the teams up. I helped them up the hill with my own hands. At dusk started on, and reached Sugar Creek about 8 P.M., having travelled nine miles. The roads were very bad."

Nine days later, temperatures fell to twelve degrees below zero, adding to the misery of the travelers. But in one way this was a blessing because the Mississippi River froze over. Now the caravans of wagons headed for Sugar Creek could cross the river on the ice.

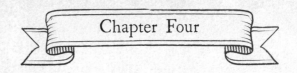

Chapter Four

Cold and Rain and Mud and Music

A young man named George Whitaker was among those who crossed the Mississippi on the ice. He and his family were recent converts from England, and he worked for Parley P. Pratt. When Parley asked him to drive a team of horses to the Rocky Mountains, he agreed to do it.

George didn't know how to drive a team of horses. Parley showed him how, telling him to let the horses "take their time" and never whip them. Then he sent George off to pick up some needed items.

"I got along very well," George wrote of the horses, "until I began to think they were not going fast enough. I gave them a little whip, which made them start up in a hurry, and the first thing I knew, they were on the full gallop. I thought they were going to get away with me, but I held on to them with all my might, until finally I brought them to. This was one of my first lessons in driving a team."

When the day came to leave Nauvoo, George put his few

possessions in a big box he had brought with him from England. "We were very busy in loading up our wagons," he wrote. "All was hurry and bustle. Brother Pratt looked at my large English box. He thought he would not be able to take it, but he finally put it into the wagon. I thought a good deal of my box and the things that were in it, but it was not long before I had to leave it behind."

George Whitaker, about 1890.

Writing about the river crossing, George said it was about noon when they started. "We had four wagons. We got down to the river and found it frozen over. We crossed over it with our wagons on the ice."

It was scary to cross the river on ice. Even though they tested the thickness of the ice, there was always the possibility that it would break. But there are no reports that anyone fell through into the frigid water.

George went on to say that they had to sweep away three to four inches of snow to set up a tent that night. They did not take time to make a fire even though it was bitter cold. "Everyone seemed to be cheerful," he wrote, "although complained a little of the cold. We ate some cold victuals and laid our beds down in the tent."

The next morning, George said, they got a late start because of the cold and snow. "The women were a long time packing up and getting their children comfortably fixed," he said. "I thought if we did not make more headway, we would be a long time getting to the Rocky Mountains, but finally we made a start."

Brigham Young reached Sugar Creek ahead of George and found that the dropping temperatures were taking a toll on the Saints there. They had just been driven from their homes in a beautiful city. It was the middle of winter. There was cold and rain and mud to endure. But the people were eager to get to their new home in the distant west. They trusted Brigham to lead them there.

Conditions at the camp were far from ideal. Helen Mar Kimball Whitney wrote, "The snow had to be cleaned away to pitch the tents, and our beds were made upon the frozen ground." Her family did not have a stove in their tent.

Even so, there was singing and dancing around the campfires among the pioneers. George Whitaker commented, "We felt as though we had been released from bondage and were free." On several nights of the week, the Saints gathered to listen to the music of a brass band or sometimes dance to fiddle music. They performed reels, polkas, and jigs, as well as square dances.

Sometimes they sat around the campfire and sang such popular songs as "Home Sweet Home" and "The Old Arm Chair."

Occasionally they came up with new songs. One of these was "The Way We Crossed the Plains":

> In a shaky wagon we ride,
> For to cross the prairie wide.
> As slowly the oxen moved along,
> We walloped them well with a good leather thong.
> The way we crossed the plains.

Brigham was happy that dancing and singing helped the Saints remain cheerful. But he himself carried a heavy sense of duty. They would be severely tested as they traveled west. There would be sickness and disease and death. He would probably be criticized and blamed for their misery. He knew some people would leave and go elsewhere.

On the other hand, he felt that going west was the only way the Church could survive. Throughout February, there were 1,800 Saints at the Sugar Creek camp. They felt privileged to be in the first

"Journeying Song," written by Eliza R. Snow.

Sugar Creek, Iowa.

Latter-day Saint company to pioneer across the vast prairie. But Brigham soon discovered a new problem. Trying to leave Nauvoo as soon as possible, hundreds of people had come without the supplies they needed. Some didn't even have enough oxen or horses to pull their wagons for long distances.

But if they went back, they would be plagued by the mobs. The Saints who were well prepared would just have to carry them along. With this setback, Heber Kimball gloomily predicted that "it would take years," not months, "to reach the mountains."

The original plans were that an advance pioneer company would travel fast over the frozen ground. They would reach the

Missouri River in four to six weeks. They would establish farms at settlements along the way, providing food for the companies of Saints who would come later.

But the ground did not stay frozen. Spring came early, and so did frequent rainstorms. Unfortunately, it turned out to be one of the wettest springs in the history of Iowa. As the Saints began their trek westward from Sugar Creek, the wagons sank deep in the mud. The horses and oxen floundered. Many possessions, like George Whitaker's box, had to be abandoned to lighten the wagons.

Instead of taking four to six weeks to reach the Missouri River, it took the struggling people more than three months. Brigham sent a message to Orson Hyde, who had stayed in Nauvoo to oversee the completion of the temple. "You have heard of a great mud hole which reaches from Nauvoo nearly to this place," he wrote. "We have at length got through it and find ourselves once more on dry land."

It didn't stay dry for very long, however. More rain came. The creeks flooded. It was too wet to build cooking fires. It was too muddy to move forward more than a mile or so a day. It was almost impossible to be warm and dry.

A worn pioneer shoe.

Despite all this, Brigham tried to remain positive. "But don't think for a moment, brethren, that we are cast down or discouraged," he wrote

Eliza R. Snow.

to Wilford Woodruff and Orson Hyde. "No! We are the happiest fellows you ever saw in the world."

Eliza R. Snow, a gifted poet, wrote a cheerful account of the journey. She mentioned that she rode with Hannah Markham, "seated in an ox wagon, on a chest with a brass kettle and a soap box for our foot stools, thankful that we are so well off."

Many people walked. Even though that was tiring, some preferred to walk because most wagons were so bouncy. They had no springs. It was said that as they rolled across the bumpy ground, they bounced so much that the motion could churn cream into butter.

Besides being uncomfortable, the wagons were packed full, making use of every bit of space. Water barrels, washtubs, pots, and churns hung on the outside. Attached to the back might be a cage of chickens. Some people built extensions on their wagons to provide more room for belongings.

Even when the going was hard, Eliza looked for the good. On February 28, she wrote, "We travelled but 4 miles and encamped in a low, truly romantic valley just large enough for our tents, wagons, etc. We arrived a little before sunset, and the prospect for the night seemed dubious enough. The ground was covered with snow, shoe deep, but our industrious men with hoes soon prepared places and pitched the tents, built wood-piles in front of them, and but a few minutes with many hands transformed the rude valley into a thriving town."

March was a month of rain and mud. The Saints made slow progress. On March 11, Eliza recorded that one of the travelers had figured they were only 55¼ miles from Nauvoo. They had barely begun the trek.

Even though they had no conveniences, the women managed to keep up some standards of home. Eliza wrote in her March 11 account, "From the dampness of my lodging or some other cause, did not rest much and feel rather indisposed. Took no breakfast, but for my dinner my good friend Sister M. brought me a slice of beautiful, white, light bread and butter that would have done honor to a more convenient bakery than an out-of-door fire in the wilderness."

Producing a loaf of beautiful, light, white bread was not a simple task. The

A loaf of bread like those the pioneers baked.

ingredients had to be kneaded on a board. Then the dough had to be put where it was warm so it would rise, near a campfire and out of the rain. Baking the loaf in the wilderness with portable equipment required skill. So it was no wonder Eliza was amazed when she was given a slice from such a loaf. But the women took pride in producing fine food in the wilderness when they could.

If March was bad, April was worse. For many people, it seemed impossible to remain hopeful. In his journal for April 9, William Huntington wrote, "Never did as many of the Church spend so disagreeable and miserable a night together before—it was very cold with high wind and hard rain all night, and no fire." Their tents, he said, were surrounded by knee-deep mud. Their animals had almost nothing to eat, and "one cow chilled to death."

"Everything is dubious for the Saints," he wrote on May 5.

Helen Mar Kimball Whitney noted, "During that time our sea biscuits, crackers, parched corn meal . . . molded." Few people were tempted to eat such food. Helen's husband, Horace K. Whitney, summed it up by saying, "Oh, what dismal days those were!"

Helen Mar Kimball Whitney.

Were the Saints' hopes doomed to drown in the rain and mud of Iowa?

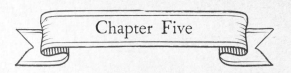

Chapter Five

The Mormon Battalion

Despite the many obstacles, Brigham and the Saints did not abandon their dream. Instead, they adjusted their plans and their expectations. They would not try to get all the Saints to the Rocky Mountains that year. When the wagon train reached a place they named Garden Grove, almost halfway between the Mississippi and the Missouri Rivers, Brigham called a halt. This was not as far west as he had hoped to be by that time. But crops must be planted for those coming later.

Besides that, it was impossible to move along such a large company of families, including children and grandparents, as fast as

Hillside pioneer cemetery at Garden Grove, Iowa.

they needed to go. At their slow pace, they would not be able to cross the western mountains before the next winter's snows.

In April, Brigham and the Twelve outlined a new plan. They would have to divide the company. A large number of the Saints would stay at Garden Grove and another way station, Mount Pisgah, to plant and tend crops there. Then a smaller, faster group of just one hundred men could make it to the mountains to prepare for the following year.

In June, with the weather finally beginning to warm up, five hundred wagons rolled onto the bluffs above the Missouri River.

Council Bluffs, Iowa, on the Missouri River.

The Saints were exhausted by the trials they had already faced. Except for a few, however, they still had confidence in Brigham.

But their situation was not good. They feared that their Missouri enemies might try to stop them. Also, they were in Indian lands now. Would the Indians be hostile? Then they heard an alarming message. It said the government's Indian agent in Council Bluffs had asked for troops to be sent to maintain peace and keep the Mormons from uniting with the Indians. There actually were United States troops in the area, Colonel Stephen W. Kearny's Army of the West. But when the leaders of the army made contact with the Saints, it was not to harass them. It was to raise volunteers. The United States was at war with Mexico. The government wanted foot soldiers. Would the Mormons supply a battalion of men for military action?

Some of the Saints saw this request as a trick by the government, an attempt to prevent them from journeying west. The government in Washington, D.C., had not helped them when they were being driven from their homes. Why should they send away desperately needed men to help the government now?

But Brigham and the other leaders saw the request as a gift from heaven. They had been seeking aid from the government, and this opportunity would pay for those men to travel west. Plus, the money the men were paid would help to finance the westward journey for the rest of the Saints.

Brigham began a spirited campaign to talk the Saints into

accepting enlistment. The men were reluctant. They feared leaving their families in a wilderness. They didn't trust the government.

But Brigham's optimism and his promises that the families would be well cared for convinced them. Around five hundred men agreed to enlist if they could be led by one of their own when possible. Their request was granted. The Mormon Battalion was formed.

Those who enlisted were promised that each man would be paid $16 a month, as well as given a clothing allowance.

When the time came for the battalion's departure, the Saints

Enrollment of the Mormon Battalion.

Farewell ball for the Mormon Battalion.

held a farewell ball, with a brass band providing the music. Most of the Saints who had been in the Nauvoo Brass Band had brought their instruments with them. Their music had lifted drooping spirits at events all along the way.

Thomas L. Kane, a friend of the Saints who had come from Washington, D.C., wrote about the evening. "A more merry dancing soul I have never seen, though the company went without refreshments," he said.

"Dancing continued until the sun dipped below the Omaha hills," he

Thomas L. Kane, advocate for the Saints.

wrote. "Silence was called, and a well cultivated mezzo-soprano voice, belonging to a young lady with a fair face and dark eyes, gave with quartet accompaniment a little song . . . touching to all earthly wanderers:

> *By the rivers of Babylon we sat down and wept.*
> *We wept when we remembered Zion."*

When the battalion marched away, musicians played "The Girl I Left behind Me," a song popular at the time. The battalion included not just men and boys but also some women who would be paid to do laundry. A few children went along, too.

The battalion headed for Fort Leavenworth, about a 170-mile march to the south in present-day Kansas. There the men received guns and other supplies, along with a clothing allowance of $42 per man. That amounted to roughly $21,000 for the battalion. Some of the money was sent back to the battalion members' families, and some went to Church leaders. It would go a long way toward paying for what the pioneers needed on the rest of the trek.

From Fort Leavenworth, the battalion marched to the southwest, arriving in Santa Fe in early October. There Lieutenant Colonel Philip St. George Cooke took command.

George Wareing with the horn he played in the Nauvoo Brass Band.

The Mormon Battalion at Winter Quarters, Nebraska.

He didn't think much of the group. He didn't like it that the group included older men, as well as a number of women and children. For instance, Jefferson Hunt was accompanied by two wives and seven children, and Elam Ludington had brought his wife and mother on the march.

At first Lieutenant Colonel Cooke wrote of the battalion, "It was enlisted too much by families; some were too old,—some feeble, and some too young; it was embarrassed by many women; it was undisciplined; it was much worn by travelling on foot, and marching from Nauvoo, Illinois; their clothing was very scant

The Mormon Battalion in California.

. . . their mules were utterly broken down . . . and animals were scarce."

By the end of their trek, however, he had come to respect and admire the courage and determination of the battalion members, and they thought better of him because of his wise leadership.

Unfortunately, some of the men and women in the group became ill from the hardships of the march. At various times "sick detachments" were sent to Fort Pueblo in what is now Colorado, where a colony of Saints from Mississippi had settled for the winter. All of the women and children, except for five wives and a handful of children, were sent along with the sick detachments.

The rest of the battalion and their families continued their march to California. They did not have to fight any battles along the way, except for what was called "The Battle of the Bulls." On December 11, 1846, near Tucson, in what is now Arizona, they were attacked by a herd of wild cattle. The men fired, killing ten to fifteen of the beasts. The battalion lost three mules, and three of the men were wounded.

By the time the battalion reached San Diego on January 29, 1847, the hostilities in California were over. Since the battalion members did not have to fight, the men spent the rest of their enlistment time serving in other ways. When their duty was fulfilled, most of them set out to return to their families. Some stayed in California, seeking employment, and several of them were at Sutter's Fort when gold was discovered there, starting the Gold Rush.

The battalion marched 2,000 miles across the plains, deserts,

Sutter's Fort near Sacramento, California.

and mountains to the Pacific Ocean. "History may be searched in vain for an equal march of infantry," Lieutenant Colonel Cooke proclaimed.

Though having the men join the battalion reduced the main pioneer group's numbers, it proved a great blessing in the end. Not only did it provide a way for many men and some of their families to travel west but it also brought in much-needed money to supply other Saints and showed that members of the Church could be loyal to their country.

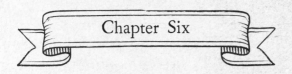

Chapter Six

The Battle of Nauvoo

While the first group of pioneers moved slowly westward, hundreds of Saints remained in Nauvoo. Some felt they were too old for the long trek west. Some were ill. Some women were expecting babies and weren't able to travel. Others were simply too poor to buy oxen and wagons and supplies.

Even though Church leaders were making plans to help get the poor out of Nauvoo, that didn't matter to their enemies. The anti-Mormons kept reminding the Saints who were still in the city about Brigham's promise that all of them would leave. Many of those who remained there, however, had no choice but to stay until help arrived.

That upset the anti-Mormon mobs. For months they had been swearing to drive out every last Latter-day Saint. In June, a group called the Convention of Hancock County Old Citizens gathered in Carthage. They were supposedly there to make plans for a Fourth of July celebration.

After discussing the situation, they decided they would

WAR DECLARED IN HANCOCK.

The last Eag'e contains a Proclamation of Peace in Hancock. Unfortunately, on the next day after the publication of the paper, a large and respectable meeting of the old settlers assembled in Carthage and declared that the time has but now arrived to commence the war.

It has been sati-factorily ascertained that there are yet in Nauvoo from 3 to 5

Warsaw Signal *showing conflicts with the Saints.*

not celebrate freedom because they were still not free from the Mormons. They would postpone their patriotic activities until the Mormons could be forced to leave.

Thomas Sharp, one of the most vocal anti-Mormons in the county, blared out the decision in a newspaper headline, saying, "War Declared in Hancock." To justify this decision, he falsely described the remaining Saints as lazy and thieving, just waiting for "an opportunity to pilfer and rob their neighbors."

A large number of armed vigilantes, people who took the law into their own hands, headed for Nauvoo. Their intention was to make sure the Mormons left, no matter what their condition.

The Saints had few defenses. The powerful Nauvoo Legion no longer existed. The state of Illinois offered little help. Before the

Saints began leaving, Governor Ford sent several hundred troops to maintain the peace. But by the time Brigham and most of the Saints left, Governor Ford had removed the state troops, believing there would be no more armed conflict.

The Saints and a number of friendly neighbors who called themselves the "new citizens" decided they had to do something on their own. They gathered what arms they could and prepared to defend themselves.

The approaching army of vigilantes was surprised by the number of new citizens who had joined with the Mormons. They stopped their march six miles south of Nauvoo to think about what they were facing. After considering the situation, they

Mobs burned the Morley settlement near Nauvoo in 1845.

decided to disband and return to their homes. However, they first tried to seal off Nauvoo, to keep the Saints from leaving the city except by ferrying across the river to Iowa.

The Saints and their new citizen friends were overjoyed that the vigilantes had stopped.

For a while there was a nervous truce. But if the Saints were to cross the river and join up with Brigham's company, they had to have money. And so they ignored the vigilantes' demand that they not leave Nauvoo except to cross the river. To earn money, a number of Saints took jobs harvesting grain in the fields outside of the city.

That led to trouble. Three of the harvesters were accused of loitering and mischief. Word spread quickly. On July 11, eight of the Mormon workers were surrounded by some eighty vigilantes led by a man named Major John McAuley. They were taken to a nearby house and forced to kneel in a ditch, where they each received twenty lashes before they were let go.

When they got back to Nauvoo, the harvesters told what had happened. One of the friendly non-Mormons, William Pickett, put together a posse of Saints and new citizens. They went after McAuley, arresting him and sixteen other men. They charged them with beating the harvesters and took them all to Nauvoo.

That action enraged the anti-Mormons. On July 14, a deputy sheriff, H. G. Ferris, reported, "Things are hot here." He had heard that "mobbers have sent messengers to every part of the country to raise a force."

Accusations flew back and forth. A Nauvoo newspaper, the *Hancock Eagle,* claimed that the Anti-Mormon Party was causing problems in order to win the August election.

In turn the anti-Mormons claimed the harvesters from Nauvoo had earned the beatings by threatening settlers. Besides, they argued, none of the men had been *severely* beaten: each had received only twenty lashes. The anti-Mormons stated again their intention to wage war against the Saints who were still in Nauvoo.

Next, the anti-Mormons took hostages in retaliation for the arrests made by Pickett's group. The anti-Mormons said it was to ensure the safe release of McAuley and his men. They kept five

A newspaper in Nauvoo.

HANCOCK EAGLE --EXTRA.

Nauvoo, Monday night, July 13, 1846,

Progress of the insurrection in Hancock! Arrest of Outlaws in their den!! Kidnapping of Citizens by the "REGULATORS"!!!— Examination of McAuley and Brattle! The city again in arms! The New Citizens call for assistance!!!

Monday night, July 13.

After the issue of our Extra on Sunday morning, news reached the city that a mob had waylaid, and, without the shadow of legal authority, made prisoners of four or five inoffensive citizens of this place, who

gang appear like men to whom scenes of violence was a congenial element.

This afternoon McAuley and Brattle were arraigned for examination before Justice Wells. The witnesses against them were the men who underwent the *lynching* on Saturday. It was proven that McAuley was present at that disgusting spectacle— that some of the movements of the lynchers were directed by him—that he "took" gun belonging to one of the laborers, and participated generally in the doings of the mob. In consideartion of this he was held to bail in the *paltry* sum of $500.

Saints captive for almost two weeks, moving them from one place to the next so they wouldn't be found. Newspaper editor Thomas Sharp declared, "The fact is, there is no peace for Hancock while a Mormon remains in it!"

Each side demanded that the other release its prisoners first. Then a judge ordered the Mormons to release McAuley and his men, which they did. The judge threw out the charges that those men had beaten the harvesters. A few days later, the Mormon hostages were also released.

By now all the citizens of Hancock County on both sides were

A pioneer-era cannon.

on alert. Although the wheat and corn in the fields were ready for harvesting, many didn't bother to do it. Everybody seemed to be waiting for a good reason to start shooting. The anti-Mormons issued a warning to the people in Nauvoo: if they left town again to go to the fields, the vigilantes would "take to the bushes and pick the Saints off."

The residents of Nauvoo appealed to Governor Ford, who sent a major and ten men from the state militia. After attempts at a peaceful resolution failed, both sides organized militia units and trained for battle.

The Saints were not prepared for a full-scale fight. For one thing, they didn't have many cannons, and so they decided to make some. As one man described it, they "cut into a steamboat's shaft, plugged it up, fixed it up on wagon wheels," and made cannon balls out of lead. The result was that this homemade equipment provided some needed firepower, even if it did not shoot accurately.

On the other hand, the vigilante posse had five proper cannons, a substantial supply of guns, and about six hundred men. This was determined by a man named Mason Brayman, who had been sent by the governor to figure out what was going on in and around Nauvoo. Mormon opponents said there were more than three thousand Saints left in Nauvoo and that they had almost as many fighting men as the vigilantes did. They said the Mormons were well-equipped with arms.

Brayman, however, found that none of that was true. The

Saints had only a small number of arms. Brayman reported to the governor that six hundred to eight hundred people were left in Nauvoo. Of these, only about two hundred were adult men who could join the fighting force.

Brayman also reported that the citizens of Nauvoo presented no real threat. The groups who had already gone west had taken everything they could haul in their wagons. There was very little left for the remaining people. There was "much sickness and many deaths," he wrote. Much of the sickness, he said, was from lack of proper food.

Brayman also told the governor, "Hundreds of poor and destitute families were encamped in tents, in huts, and covered wagons on the opposite side of the river." He said people in Illinois were worried that the "approach of winter would drive [the Saints] back to the city, reduced to pauperism and theft for subsistence."

In spite of their poor condition, the Saints in Nauvoo formed their battle lines and waited for their enemies to attack. The women baked bread to feed the soldiers. Some gathered with their children in a house close to the temple. There were guards nearby, and they thought they would be safer there.

Others, including Emma Smith, Joseph's widow, left the area. She and her five children boarded a riverboat and joined relatives upriver.

The makeshift armies scurried around to find locations that would give them an advantage in a fight. There were attacks and counterattacks by both sides. Crowds of people gathered to watch the battle.

The invaders kept up the pressure on Nauvoo. The Nauvoo forces made valiant efforts at defense but were outnumbered. Over three days of fighting, there were some deaths and even more injuries, but not as many as might be expected given all of the shooting.

Later, Governor Ford reported to the Illinois House of Representatives, "It appears that the remarkable fact of so few being killed and wounded on either side, can only be accounted for by supposing great unskillfulness in the use of arms, and by the very safe distance which the parties kept from each other."

Emma Smith holding her son David Hyrum Smith, about 1845.

Eventually the battle ended when both sides ran short of ammunition. The Saints in Nauvoo waved a white flag, signaling they were ready to surrender and work out a peace treaty. Representatives from both sides met to sign what they called "Articles of Accommodation, Treaty and Agreement." That ended the fighting.

Militia driving Saints from Nauvoo.

Under the terms of the agreement, the remaining Saints in Nauvoo were to surrender their arms and cross the river to Iowa as soon as possible. A few were allowed to stay in order to sell what property was left. The Saints were required to give the keys of the temple to a committee that was negotiating the surrender. When the surrender was complete, the militia from Carthage entered the city.

The members of the Carthage militia, who had agreed not to molest the Saints further, did not keep their word. Soldiers seized some citizens who were trying to leave and dumped them into the waters of the Mississippi in mock baptisms. They searched wagons and houses, tearing up floors and rummaging through chests and trunks.

"The mob kept up one continual stream through the temple," Thomas Bullock wrote, "ringing the bell, shouting, and hallooing." "A mob preacher ascended to the top of the tower and, standing outside, proclaimed with a loud voice, 'Peace, Peace, Peace to all the inhabitants of the earth, now the Mormons are driven.'"

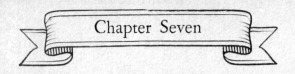

Chapter Seven

The Miracle of the Quails

On the west side of the Mississippi River, the homeless Saints huddled in whatever flimsy shelter they could put together. The weather in late September had turned cold and rainy. Some people suffered fevers and chills. A baby was born, only to die a few hours later. The people shared what food and provisions they had, but their situation was desperate. If they did not get help soon, many would perish.

They didn't know it, but even before the Battle of Nauvoo ended, help was on the way. Brigham and the forward company of pioneers on the Missouri River had not forgotten them. The Saints there had been busy since they stopped. They harvested hay for their animals. They built cabins to live in. And they appointed a man named Orville M. Allen to lead a relief company to go back for the Saints left behind.

In calling for help, Brigham said, "I have felt sensibly there was a good deal of suffering among the saints in Nauvoo, as there has been amongst us, but the Lord God who has fed us all the day

long, has his care still over us and when the Saints are chastened
enough, it will cease. I have never believed the Lord would suffer
a general massacre of this people by a mob. If ten thousand men
were to come against us, and no other way was open for our deliv-
erance, the earth would swallow them up."

Camp at Keokuk, Iowa, of Saints expelled from Nauvoo.

Brother Allen and another man in a separate group, James
Murdock, were instructed to return to the banks of the Mississippi
to save as many Saints there as they could. It would be a journey
of 327 miles back through the mud of Iowa. They set off with as
many wagons and animals to pull them as could be spared. Brother

Allen arrived at what were being called "the misery camps" at Montrose, Iowa, on October 7.

More than three hundred people huddled there—men, women, and children. They were barely surviving. Their main food was corn, which they ate boiled or parched. For water, they drank from the river. Some had already died. Many of those remaining suffered from disease and exposure to the elements.

Brother Allen and his companions arrived first. They immediately began to organize the despairing people into a traveling company. With the animals they had brought and whatever equipment the Saints had, they were able to put together 28 serviceable wagons. These were sufficient to carry 157 people and their few belongings westward. But they had only meager food and limited supplies. They had been weakened by the ordeals they had suffered.

Then on October 9, a miracle occurred. Thomas Bullock wrote that those in the ragged camp were amazed to see flocks of quail swoop overhead and then settle to the ground.

"This morning we had a direct manifestation of the mercy and goodness of God, in a miracle being performed in the Camp," he wrote. "A large, or rather several large flocks of quails, flew into camp. Some fell on the wagons, some under, some on the breakfast tables. The boys and the brethren ran about after them and caught them alive with their hands. Men who were not in the church marveled at the sight."

"The boys caught about twenty alive," he reported. "Every

The miracle of the quails.

man, woman and child had quails to eat for their dinner and after dinner the flocks increased in size." And that was not all. "The quails flew around the camp, many delighted in it. Then all the flock would rise, fly around our camp again a few rods off and then would alight again and close to the camp. This was repeated more than half a dozen times."

In this way, the Saints were able to have fresh meat at the start of their journey.

"The brethren and sisters praised God and glorified his name," Thomas recorded.

Another good thing happened that day. Brigham and the Twelve had appointed a few men to linger in Nauvoo to take care of any final business before leaving for good. These trustees came to the camp as the wagons were readying to depart. They brought shoes and clothing, as well as salt, molasses, and salt pork.

Brother Murdock's relief train was not far behind the first one, and all the suffering Saints by the river finally had transportation to cross Iowa. The last departing group began their trek west with lifted spirits and hope. They couldn't help but remember the miracle that occurred when Moses led the children of Israel out of Egypt as told in Exodus 16:13–15:

"And it came to pass, that at even the quails came up, and covered the camp: and in the morning the dew lay round about the host.

"And when the dew that lay was gone up, behold, upon the face of the wilderness there lay a small round thing, as small as the hoar frost on the ground.

"And when the children of Israel saw it, they said one to another, It is manna: for they wist not what it was. And Moses said unto them, This is the bread which the Lord hath given you to eat."

A quail.

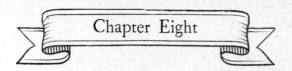
Winter Quarters

Brigham had hoped to lead some of the Saints all the way to the Rocky Mountains in 1846. However, he hadn't planned on so many obstacles along the way. The sticky mud of Iowa slowed them down. More than five hundred of their strongest men and

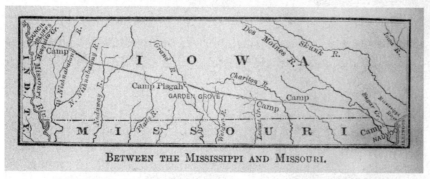

BETWEEN THE MISSISSIPPI AND MISSOURI.

The Mormon Trail between the Mississippi River and the Missouri.

boys went off to form the Mormon Battalion. Then the forward company had to wait for those left behind to be rescued.

By the time the groups were reunited, it was too late in the year to go on. Winter was close at hand. The Saints could not continue their trek until the next year's snows were past.

Their stopping point was the Missouri River. A large number of the Saints crossed the river onto land that belonged to the Otoe and Omaha Indians. Other people stayed on the Iowa side of the river. That land belonged to the Potawatomi Indians.

The Indians understood what it was like to be hated and driven from their homes. They allowed the Mormons to stay. It was good land with fertile soil. There was plenty of grass for their thousands of animals, which included cattle, sheep, mules, and horses.

The Saints immediately surveyed the area and built shelters. Soon on the west side of the river arose what Zina Huntington called a "city of log huts." They named it Winter Quarters. By

Settlement built by Saints at Kanesville, Iowa.

Christmas, approximately 3,500 Saints were gathered there. Thousands more settled on the Iowa side of the river. In all, about 12,000 pioneers were strung out across the prairie, living in cabins, huts, and dugouts.

The trek so far had been difficult and demanding. Many of the Saints were unhappy. Food was inadequate. They had little more than corn bread and

Mill built by the Saints at Winter Quarters, in present-day Nebraska.

salt bacon to eat. Sometimes there was milk, and occasionally fresh meat.

But not much fruit and few fresh vegetables were available. Because of this lack in their diet, people got sick from a disease called scurvy. They also suffered from lung diseases and various fevers. There was very little medical care. Some died, not only from disease but also from the other hardships of their lives.

One person in great demand during these bad times was Patty Sessions, often known as "Mother Sessions." Patty was a midwife who had delivered numerous babies in Nauvoo and on the westward trek. She also cared for those who were ill. Excerpts from her diary show how busy she was. She spent a lot of her time delivering babies, which is what she meant when she wrote about putting a sister to bed. In January 1847 she recorded:

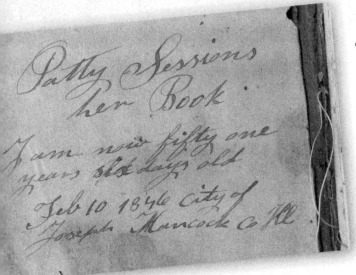

Journal kept by Patty Sessions.

Tuesday 5. I have been out all night. Had no sleep. Put Sister Alexander to bed. Came home. Wrote a letter to Mother. . . . .

Wednesday 6. I have baked some mince pies. Called to sister Cyntha . . . Dikes.

Thursday 7. Put her to bed with her 20th child. I have visited the sick.

Friday 8. Put Loiza, Adaline, and Melissa all to bed in 6 hours and a half.

Saturday 9. P. G. came home. Visited the sick.

Sunday 10. Visited the sick.

Monday 11. Called to Sister Empy. Staid all night. She got better.

Tuesday 12. Brigham, Heber, and wives came here on a visit.

Wednesday 13. Put Sister Hall to bed. Visited many sick.

Thursday 14. Put Sister Knight to bed. Miscarriage yesterday. Visited the sick today. Spun some yarn for a comforter.

Friday 15. Put Harriet F. Wicksome to bed. Sister Empy sent for me. Child born before I got there.

Patty's compassion shows through when she speaks of a sister whose conduct she did not like:

> *Tuesday 26.* Called to Hannah Jones. Talked to her for her bad conduct. Then I went to the bishop to have a bedstead fixed up for her and to make her comfortable, although I thought she was a bad woman. Yet she lay on the ground and about to be confined and I pitied her.
>
> *Wednesday 27.* Visited her again. Set her son to fix her bedstead.
>
> *Thursday 28.* Put William Wicks's wife to bed. Called on for counsel by Sabre Grible. Called on again to visit Hannah.

Patty drew inspiration and comfort from Brigham as a leader. "Brother Brigham blessed the people," she wrote following a Sunday service. "I felt his blessing even to the healing of my body. Have been better ever since."

Patty became quite ill later. Brigham and Heber came to bless her. Feeling that death was near, she asked them to make a record of where they buried her. In her diary she wrote, "Brigham said they must all hold onto me as long as I breathed and 15 minutes after I had done breathing." Eventually she regained her health and went on with her nursing and midwifery.

Patty was only one person, however. She could not take care of all of those who needed nursing. Lorenzo Snow, who later became president of the Church, wrote about conditions at one of the Mormon way stations in Iowa called Mount Pisgah:

"The latter part of July and August witnessed a general and

Elder Lorenzo Snow.

almost universal scene of sickness," he explained. "Well persons could not be found to take care of the sick; it was indeed a distressing scene. A great number of deaths occurred, and it was very often very difficult to get their bodies decently interred. In one or two instances bodies were put into the ground without any coffin or box. Scarcely a family escaped sickness and very few where death did not make an inroad."

It was no wonder that some people grew discouraged and filled with doubt. Was Brigham the right leader to follow? The future seemed uncertain, and the wish to find an easier life, away from hardship, was tempting.

Brigham knew people were murmuring. He knew they had good reasons to do so. But he did not attempt to soothe them. He had suffered along with the rest, while also shouldering the burden of leadership.

In a December sermon, he scolded the Saints. "You must stop," he declared. He said they should cease their backbiting and speaking evil of him and the other leaders.

"Brother Joseph, being a very merciful man, bore with these things until it took his life," he said, "but I will not do it." He announced that those who were unhappy with him should go on back to Missouri if they chose. Those who stayed must turn away from sinful behavior and repent.

For two weeks, that was the tone of his preaching. He felt it accomplished what the Saints needed. In a letter to Charles C. Rich, he said, "We have had quite a reformation at this place of late." He spoke of "good feelings prevailing" among the people.

Brigham could be harsh, but when the lecturing was finished, he could show a lighter side. One evening after a meeting, he allowed several musicians to come and play music for dancing. The people were delighted. They relaxed and enjoyed themselves. At the end of the dance, they joined in singing a hymn called, "Come, Let Us Anew Our Journey Pursue." The words reflected their renewed determination.

Mount Pisgah, a pioneer way station in Iowa.

Brigham realized that to keep their spirits up, the Saints sorely needed some of the things that had made life good in Nauvoo. That meant not only work to do but also recreation and spiritual uplifting.

Not long after the evening of

Lucy Mack Smith, mother of the Prophet Joseph Smith.

dancing, Brigham told of a dream he had. In the dream, he saw Joseph Smith talking to his mother, Lucy Mack Smith. She was reading a pamphlet, and Joseph asked, "Have you got the word of God there?"

"Yes," she answered.

Then Joseph said, "I think you will be sick of that pretty soon."

Brigham interpreted the dream as meaning that more was needed than the scriptures and past revelations. Three days after the dream, on January 14, 1847, he sat down and wrote out what he called "the Word and Will of the Lord." Heber Kimball called this document a revelation, the first recorded since Joseph was murdered. It eventually became section 136 of the Doctrine and Covenants.

The revelation covered many subjects. It began by describing how the Camp of Israel should be structured for the coming journey: "Let the companies be organized with captains of hundreds, captains of fifties, and captains of tens, with a president and his two counselors at their head, under the direction of the Twelve Apostles."

The revelation went on to say that each company would be responsible for the needs of the people within it. They would take care of "the poor, the widows, and the fatherless." They would see that the families of the Mormon Battalion men had what they needed. Also, each company would make its own preparations for continuing the journey.

The people were admonished to stop arguing with each other. They should avoid the sins of contention and drunkenness and should return things they borrowed or found. And then the revelation said, "If thou art merry, praise the Lord with singing, with music, with dancing, and with a prayer of praise and thanksgiving."

That uplifted the spirits of the Saints. It also raised Brigham in the eyes of the people. The revelation likened the Saints to the ancient Israelites, promising that the arm of the Lord would protect and save them. Most of those who had faltered once again put their faith in Brigham as their leader.

The time to start their spring journey was approaching. As they prepared, the Saints often took time to praise the Lord with singing and dancing. A young woman

Mary Haskin Parker Richards.

named Mary Haskin Parker Richards recorded one incident in her diary. On January 26, 1847, she said Brigham was her partner for a sprightly dance at a party. "Sister Mary," he said after the dance ended, "you have learned me. I am very much obliged to you."

He often encouraged the people to enjoy themselves while they could, before their challenging journey began again. "You may dance all night," he told them, "there is no harm in it."

Sometime later he said, "All music is in heaven, all enjoyment is of the Lord." He felt that dancing was important, just like growing food and building houses.

But it was not all dancing and music. Although these settlements were temporary, the Saints still needed a government to maintain order and assign work details. The Church high councils operated as town councils. They levied taxes to pay for a police force, and they encouraged the establishment of schools.

Because the Saints were staying where they were for the winter, they began trading with permanent settlers living nearby. They traded whatever they didn't need for vegetables, grain, hogs, and supplies they could take with them when they finally headed west.

Some of the young men cut down willows along the riverbanks to make baskets to trade or sell in the nearby settlements. Some made such handy items as washboards. Brigham set up a company to build a gristmill to grind corn and wheat. He also organized a mail service so the various communities could stay in touch with one another.

In addition to everything else, Brigham sent some of the

A pioneer-era gristmill used to grind such grains as corn and wheat.

apostles off to England. They were to oversee missionary work and emigration activities there.

The Saints' faith and commitment to their cause led some of them to view their situation positively. One woman wrote to her family back home: "The land is far from being level here, but the hills are really beautiful, far more so to me, than the level land could be. If you could sail up the river and take a peep at our place, you would say it was romantic and grand, notwithstanding the log huts."

As spring approached, temperatures warmed and plants started to grow. Some Saints would need to stay for another year, but most were ready to move on. They would leave behind what they had built for the use of those who came later. Their permanent home was still far ahead, deep in the mountains of the American West.

Log cabin similar to those built by the pioneers.

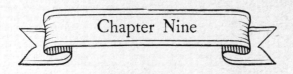

Chapter Nine

The Vanguard

In April, it was time for the first pioneer company to journey on to its final destination. This group would be made up of 144 men. The number was symbolic, with twelve men representing each of the twelve tribes of Israel. They were picked because of their abilities and included farmers and blacksmiths and carpenters. All of these skills would be needed in the new city they would build.

Most in this first group were youthful and full of energy. Brigham and Heber, at 46, were among the oldest. Also in this first group were three women and two children.

Brigham had not planned on that. But Harriet Decker Young, wife of Brigham's younger brother Lorenzo, objected to staying behind. She had asthma, and the river air was bad for her. She wanted to go with her husband on the trail, believing that being left behind would mean death from sickness.

Brigham did not want her to go. But Lorenzo said he would stay behind if Harriet could not join him.

Roll of Compy Nᵒ 1

Brigham Young
Heber C Kimball
Orson Hyde
P. P. Pratt
Orson Pratt
John E Page
John Taylor
Amasa Lyman
George A Smith
Willard Richards
Newel K Whitney
George Miller

Page 1 of the roll of the first company to leave Winter Quarters.

How could a lone woman travel with all those men? Brigham decided to allow at least two more women to travel with them. One of his wives was Clara Decker Young, who was Harriet's daughter. If Clara went along, she and Harriet would be good company for each other. Brigham also gave permission for one of Heber Kimball's wives, Ellen Sanders Kimball, to go. In addition, Harriet's two young sons, Isaac and Lorenzo, were allowed to join the group.

Clara Young suffered from asthma, like her mother, Harriet. But even though the two women were somewhat frail, there is nothing recorded that shows they were a burden on the trek.

Harriet had grown up in New Hampshire and Massachusetts. At seventeen she taught school in a town about four miles from

Harriet Decker Young, Clara Decker Young, and Ellen Sanders Kimball, of the first pioneer company.

the Hill Cumorah. There she met and married Isaac Decker and gave birth to several children, including Clara. The family moved to Ohio, where they learned of the Saints and joined the Church. That led them to Nauvoo, where Harriet and Isaac's marriage ended. Harriet later married Brigham's brother Lorenzo.

Clara, daughter of Harriet and Isaac, was a rather sickly child. To make matters worse, when she was three years old, a terrible accident happened. Clara wandered too close to where her father was chopping wood, and she was hit in the head with his ax. Her parents thought at first she was dead, but she survived, although for a year she did not speak. As she grew, she made a complete recovery. She became one of Brigham's plural wives when she was sixteen years old.

Ellen Sanders was thirteen when she immigrated to the United States with her family from Norway in 1824, settling in Indiana. A year later, her mother died, followed almost immediately by her father. Ellen and her siblings went their own ways, and she became a hired girl for another family.

In 1842 she met some Saints and joined the Church. Soon after that, she moved to Nauvoo, where she became acquainted with the Heber Kimball family. On January 7, 1846, she became one of Heber's plural wives. It was only a month later that they left Nauvoo and started the long journey westward.

Harriet, Clara, and Ellen became known as "Utah's three pioneer women."

By the time of departure, one of the 144 men chosen to be in the first company to leave Winter Quarters fell ill, and so only 143 started out. There were 70 wagons and carriages in the train, with 93 horses, 52 mules, and 66 oxen. The pioneer company also took with them 19 cows, 17 dogs, and some chickens. In addition, they pulled a leather boat for crossing rivers, as well as a cannon.

The first wagons left Winter Quarters on April 5, 1847. This company was large for a wagon train, but it was small compared to the number of Saints who were left behind. The plan was that these first pioneers would travel fast and mark the trail for the thousands who would travel later.

Brigham did not go with the wagons that left first on April 5. He stayed behind to lead the Church's general conference on April 6. In his sermon that day he said, "I am anxious to leave this place and be about my errand." Always a doer, he told them, "The principle of eternally preaching and never practicing is folly."

A wagon train near the Salt Lake Valley.

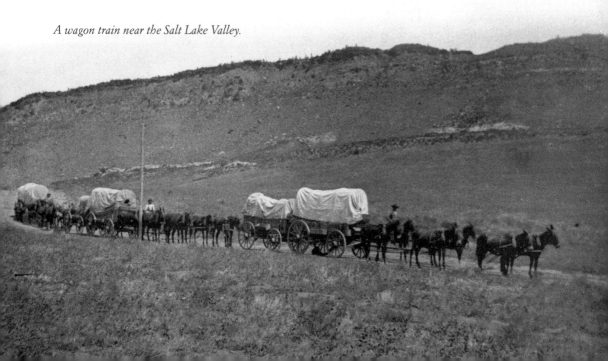

He gave instructions on what the Saints should do in his absence. "Pray for yourselves, and your enemies," he said. "Pray that God may soften their hearts until we are out of their grasp."

After fulfilling his conference duties at Winter Quarters, Brigham caught up with the members of the first company. The next leg of the journey was a stretch of very rough country, including a wet, soggy swamp. Wagons bogged down in the mire. No matter how hard the oxen and horses strained, they could not budge the wagons. The men attached ropes. They yanked. The animals tugged. Together, they succeeded in getting through the swamp.

When the company halted for the day, the men inspected the animals to make sure they hadn't been hurt in the ordeal. The Saints gathered grass for the creatures to eat. They had to take good care of the animals. The journey could not continue without their strength.

On Sunday, April 11, Brigham called the travelers together. He said he would return to Winter Quarters the next day with seven other apostles in the group. They wanted to welcome John Taylor and Parley Pratt, who had been on missions in England. Brother Taylor had purchased scientific equipment there, things the Saints would need on the journey to their new home.

Heber Kimball then spoke to the assembled pioneers. He said he hoped there would be no hunting or fishing on the Sabbath because "this was a day set apart for the service of the Lord and not for trivial amusement."

Elder John Taylor.

Elder Parley P. Pratt.

After the meeting, some of the men spent the day writing letters for their families. It might be their last chance for a long time to send letters, which would be carried back to Winter Quarters by Brigham and other Church officials.

During the absence of the leaders, the company was to continue on to the Platte River. They would follow this stream for hundreds of miles. Most of the other groups of people heading west traveled along the south bank of the river. Because of where they started and because of recent experiences with mob violence and persecution, the Saints mostly stayed on the less-traveled north bank. They wanted to keep distance between themselves

The trail from Winter Quarters to the Platte River.

and the many others going west. The route they followed became known as the Mormon Trail.

Thomas Bullock went back to Winter Quarters with Brigham's group. After he returned to the advance group with a small company, he told of a surprise visit from a group of Indians. Thomas was hitching cattle to his wagon when "four Omaha Indians came rushing down" toward them, stampeding the cattle.

To calm the situation, the company gave the Indians some of their bread. The Indians wanted more, and Thomas wrote of the riders, "One had the boldness to come to my wagon and attempt to take the front of my wagon cover to make him a head dress, but I repelled him, and he went away in anger."

This incident was unusual. Most encounters between the pioneers and Indians were peaceful. Like the Saints, many of the

Indians they met had been pushed off land they considered their own. They were suspicious of these travelers. Would they try to take over the Indians' new land? Would they kill the animals and plants on which they depended for survival? The Saints, for the most part, tried to be considerate of their use of resources and offered presents to Indians as they passed through their lands.

Back in Winter Quarters, Brigham and his companions prepared to rejoin the advance company. Brigham and Willard Richards went to William Clayton and told him to be ready to join the vanguard group in half an hour. But William was sick with what he called "rheumatism of the face," caused by an infected tooth.

Nevertheless, William wanted to be included in the forward company of Saints. His family helped him gather his clothes and some supplies to prepare for the long trip. William would be a scribe and historian during the journey.

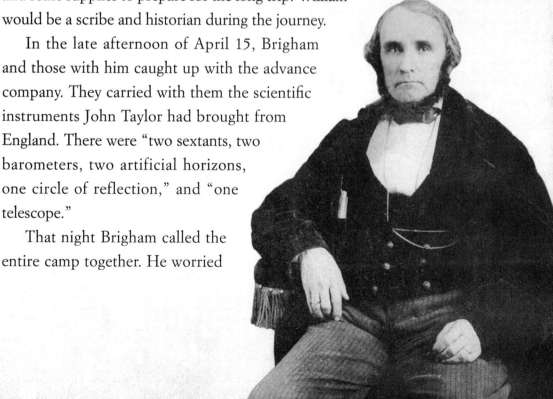

William Clayton.

In the late afternoon of April 15, Brigham and those with him caught up with the advance company. They carried with them the scientific instruments John Taylor had brought from England. There were "two sextants, two barometers, two artificial horizons, one circle of reflection," and "one telescope."

That night Brigham called the entire camp together. He worried that Indians were being stirred up to steal supplies and animals from them, and he cautioned everyone to be diligent in their guard duties. He counseled them to be "faithful, humble and prayerful" and said they "should go to bed early, rest on Sabbath, and go in such a manner as to claim the blessing of Heaven."

Thomas Bullock.

He set up nine rules he expected them to obey, and they were to be read to the camp each Sunday. Thomas Bullock recorded them:

1st. Every morning at 5 o'clock, horn to be blown, then every man to arise and pray, attend to cattle and breakfast, and be ready to start at 7 o'clock.

2nd. Every extra man travel on off side of his wagon, with his gun loaded, over his shoulder; every driver to have his in wagon, ready for a moment's warning—with a piece of leather on the nipple, or in the pan of his gun—having caps and powder flasks ready.

3rd. Halt for an hour about noon, every man must have his dinner ready cooked.

4th. Camp to halt for the night in a circle. Horses fastened inside (and cattle when necessary).

5th. Horn to be blown at ½ past 8 every night, when

Every morning at 5 o clock, Horn to be blown, then every man to arise & pray, attend to

" Every extra man travel on off side of his *wagon*, with his gun loaded, over his Sh

for a moments ~~wagon~~ *warning* - with a piece of leather on the nipple, or in the Pan of hi

" Halt for an hour about noon, every man must have his dinner ready cooked,

Camp to halt for the night in a circle, Horses fastened inside, / & cattle when nec

Letter from Thomas Bullock to his wife Henrietta, outlining camp rules, May 10, 1847.

every man (except the guard for the night) must retire to his wagon, pray, and be in bed by 9, when all fires must be put out.

6th. The camp to travel in close order, under their captains of tens, and no man to leave the camp 20 rods, without orders from his captain.

7th. Every man to feel as much care and interest in his brother's cattle, and preserving them, as he would of his own—but indulge no man in idleness.

8th. Every man to have his guns and pistols, in perfect order.

9th. The tens to keep together, the cannon bring up the rear, the company organized. Travel with it, and see that nothing is left behind at stopping places.

The next morning, Brigham organized the group and reminded them of the rules. He didn't want anyone along who wasn't fully committed. Heber admonished the group: If they couldn't obey the rules without complaining, they should turn back immediately.

At last the company started on their way. That night was bitterly cold. When the bugle woke the camp the next morning at 5 o'clock, the water in their buckets was covered with an inch of ice. It was a reminder of the difficulties they would face on the trek. They knew they might suffer from hunger, illness, fatigue, and backbreaking work. There would be danger.

Some must have longed to be with their families. But they were also eager to move on, and their faith carried them forward to the west.

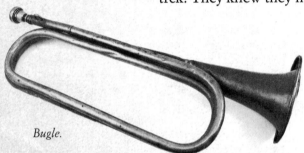

Bugle.

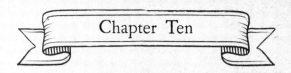
Buffalo!

The morning of April 19, 1847, dawned pleasant and promising. It was easy traveling that day. There was plenty of water, with good weather the whole way. The pioneers logged about twenty miles, and at night they camped near the banks of the Platte River. Some of the men went fishing at one of the many small lakes in the area. They came back with, as one man reported, "a snapping turtle, four small turtles, one duck, two small cat fish, and two creek suckers."

Two days later, Heber Kimball recorded, "The country is beautiful and pleasing to the eye of the traveler, notwithstanding there is only the same kind of scenery from day to day, namely on the left the majestic Platte with its muddy waters." But they couldn't always see the river, which was "frequently hid from view by the many handsome cottonwood groves, before and behind, on the right and left a vast, level prairie."

The Platte River may have been majestic, but it could also be treacherous. "It is the most singular river I ever beheld," Wilford

Woodruff wrote. "It is from three quarters to a mile wide, and its shores and bed one universal body of quicksand. It is a rapid stream, yet in many places a person can wade across. Frequently the whole bed of the river is covered with but a few inches of water, and at other places it is deep and rapid."

The quicksand made travel dangerous. "Horses and cattle can walk down to the edge of the river and drink, like walking on the edge of a smooth sea beach," Wilford explained. But "sometimes while walking on the apparent hard beach or bed of the river a man or horse will suddenly sink into the quicksand." Wilford

North Platte River Crossing.

Wagons were circled at night.

recorded, "Many men and horses have been lost in this way on the Platte."

Brigham did not mention these dangers when he took time to write a letter to his wife Mary Ann and the children back in Winter Quarters. "The camp is in good health and first rate spirits," he wrote. "They have never felt better in their lives. I think my health has very much improved yesterday and today. You mentioned in your letter that you heard I lay on the ground the night I left home. I did, but do not think it hurt me. But when I arrived in camp, I found myself completely tired out."

The Saints' first encounter with a large group of Indians came when the wagon train passed near a Pawnee village. The pioneers offered gifts of attractive trinkets, as well as gunpowder, tobacco, and flour. The Indians were friendly, but they warned the travelers not to kill their buffalo. They also advised them to turn back.

From what the Indians said, the Saints suspected that Missourians or traders had been influencing them against the Mormons.

When Brigham addressed the Saints at a worship service the next Sunday, he said, "We do not anticipate any attack by the Indians to kill any of the men, but to steal horses." The men appointed as guards were to see that this did not happen.

Brigham also addressed the complaining that was happening in the group. With a bit of humor, he appointed a "chief grumbler." He said, "Anyone who wants to murmur, go to Henry G. Sherwood, who will do the business for them." Henry, overseer of food and supplies, seemed amused by his new responsibility.

Norton Jacob commented in his journal that the new ruling had an "excellent effect in putting a check upon some fractious persons," especially one man who always seemed to be arguing. "But after this he was tolerable decent."

That night and the following day, Brigham's prediction about Indians came true. A few who desperately wanted horses managed to steal two, despite the guards. Brigham and several other men went off in search of them, but they did not get the horses back.

Conditions along the trail began to change now, more than two hundred miles from Winter Quarters. Trees became scarce. That meant there was less fuel for campfires. They either had to eat their meals cold or use whatever fuel was available.

William Clayton wrote, "The camp have found a good substitute for wood in the dried buffalo dung which lies on the ground here in great plenty, and makes a good fire when properly

A wagon train at Chimney Rock, in what is now Nebraska.

managed." For many miles across the open plains, buffalo chips were an important source of fuel for their cooking fires.

Another unpleasant condition was the dust. Stirred up by the rolling wagon wheels and the animals, it coated everything and made it hard just to breathe. It was almost impossible for the travelers to keep themselves and their clothes clean.

In addition, a cold wind took the temperature down to freezing. "Every man wants his overcoat on and a buffalo robe over it," William Clayton wrote. Nobody recorded how the three women—Ellen, Clara, and Harriet—and Harriet's two young sons faced the bitter weather. But it is certain they suffered right along with the men.

On May 1, a cold, windy day, the members of the company saw their first buffalo. The animals were huge and wild-looking. The herds were so large that a dreadful stink rose from them. Nevertheless, the pioneers were fascinated.

William Clayton described them: "The color of the back and about half way down the sides is a light brown. The rest is a very dark brown. The shoulder appears slightly rounding and humped. When running, the large shaggy head hangs low down." He compared the buffalo to farm animals. "They canter like any ox or cow, but appear far more cumbersome and heavy," he wrote, "on account of the long, thick matty hair."

Several of the camp's hunters pursued the herd. They killed ten animals and distributed the meat throughout the camp. Everyone had a good supper of roast buffalo that night. They described the meat as being sweet and tender like veal.

A buffalo on the prairie.

Unfortunately, the pioneers' digestive systems were not used to fresh meat. The next day George A. Smith wrote, "I ate heartily of buffalo meat, and was routed out very early by its effect." Many people became quite ill until their stomachs adjusted to this new item on their menu.

For the next few days, the wagon train moved slowly. The people wanted to watch the buffalo and the hunters who went after them. In one incident, the hunters were closing in when a barking dog chased an antelope into the herd. The dog pursued it until he got very close to the buffalo. Then the dog apparently had second thoughts about the whole thing. Giving up his barking, he turned and retreated swiftly, much to the amusement of those watching.

The people back at the wagons were somewhat anxious about the hunting. The hunters were inexperienced when it came to buffalo. They had all heard stories of how ferocious the animals were when being chased. Unfortunately, it usually took more than one shot to bring down one of the huge beasts, and so the hunters needed to stay close to their prey.

Heber Kimball almost got into real trouble when he went in to finish off a wounded buffalo cow. He fired a shot that killed her, but he had to fire over the head of his horse, which then panicked and plunged away. Heber, who had let go of the reins so he could manage his gun, was almost knocked off the horse.

The other hunters watched helplessly. Heber was an excellent horseman, however, and eventually regained control of his mount.

killed, either antelope, buffalo, or any thing else, "*for,*
said he, "*my opinion is, that if we do slay when we*
not need, we will need when we cannot slay".—*L*

Horace Whitney quoting President Brigham Young.

For the next several days, the men brought in more buffalo that they had killed. But Brigham was worried that the enthusiastic hunters were getting greedy. He issued a new ruling. "There should be no more game killed until such time as it should be needed," he said, "for it was a sin to waste life and flesh." He reminded the Saints again and again, "If we do slay when we do not need, we will need when we cannot slay."

Sometimes the pioneers' fascination with the vast herds led them to neglect their camp duties and ride out to the buffalo. They did not keep a good watch over their own cattle. At one time Brigham lost his patience.

"Yesterday there was no one with the cows," he scolded, "and they started twice to go to the buffalo, and I had to run my horse twice to bring them back, in doing which I lost a good telescope. I did not know then that Erastus Snow was the driver for that time. If I had, I should have known that he would not go out of his road one rod, he is so lazy."

Brigham and Erastus had a heated conversation about this. Eventually Erastus admitted his error, promising he would do better. Brigham's costly telescope that John Taylor brought from England was eventually found, and things calmed down.

Hunting buffalo.

One problem with having so many buffalo around was that they ate all the grass, leaving none for the pioneers' animals. At one camp, Brigham and Heber walked out to look the situation over. They saw the grass nibbled right down to the dirt. There was little left to feed their horses and oxen.

William Clayton reported seeing hundreds of dead buffalo on the prairie. He did not know if they starved to death or were shot by hunters that had passed before.

The stench of their rotting carcasses sickened some of the pioneers. Harriet Young, who was expecting a baby, recorded, "I was very sick all day in consequence of taking the scent of a dead buffalo." Lorenzo gave her some medicine, and she got better. But she still felt discouraged. "It is a lonesome country to me to travel

Buffalo bones on the prairie.

through," she wrote. "There is no flowers and little or no timber."

Farther west, the buffalo herds dwindled. Very likely they had moved east to look for more grass. There was evidence in the area that great herds had been there at one time or another. Thomas Bullock recorded, "The valley we traveled through this day may be called 'The Valley of Dry Bones,' because of the immense number of bleached buffalo bones."

But the pioneers continued west, one dusty day after another, toward their new home.

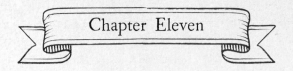
Perils on the Trail

As their wagons creaked along, the pioneers sometimes saw signs of Indians being nearby. On May 4, 1847, Brigham called a meeting in which he warned the men against leaving the camp to hunt. If they did, he predicted that "some of them would be caught by the Indians and if not killed would be severely abused." He said those who disobeyed the camp rules must be punished, and each man should "seek his neighbor's welfare as much as his own."

Even though the pioneers did travel past what they thought were Indian war parties, there usually were no problems. But some Indians set prairie fires. The flames burned the grass the pioneers needed for their animals.

At one point they came to a stretch of prairie that Thomas Bullock said burned "like a roaring furnace." They decided to go back a mile to camp for the night. "The wind blew the ashes of the burnt grass in all directions," Thomas wrote, "which soon caused

Prairie fire.

us to look like [chimney] sweeps." But, he wrote, "by washing, after our halt, we were enabled to discern each other again."

One day the fires came so close that Brigham ordered the entire wagon train to ford the river to a small island. They were safe there, and there was also grass to feed their hungry animals.

When the flames died down, the pioneers were able to cross the river again and continue on their way. But the fires and herds of buffalo had left hardly any grass for their animals. "The feed is so short and teams so weak," Wilford Woodruff wrote, "that we are unable to travel but a short portion of the day."

Several journals mention the disagreeable weather as they traveled along. "The evening was cold, with strong wind from the northwest," Howard Egan wrote on May 9. "President Young ate supper with H. C. Kimball. Ellen tried to bake some bread, but could not, the wind blew so. I have to sleep on a chest in the front part of the wagon, crossways, and cannot stretch myself nor keep the clothes over me. It was so cold tonight, and the wind blowing in the wagon, so I went to bed with Brothers King and Cushing."

Along the way, William Clayton had time to think about something that bothered him. As a historian of the camp, he had been recording the miles traveled. It was important to measure distances so they could send information back to those who would come later. But they had nothing to accurately measure the miles.

At first, they just guessed how far they had come each day, but the estimates differed. One day William measured a wheel on a wagon belonging to Heber Kimball and figured it made 360 complete turns in a mile. He began walking alongside the wagon, counting each complete turn. That gave a fairly accurate count of miles traveled, but he found that the counting was boring and the turning of the wheel made him dizzy.

Then he had an idea. It involved wooden gears being attached to the hub of a wheel. He didn't know how to make the contraption. Orson Pratt listened to what he said and drew a design for the device. He showed it to Appleton Harmon, who had knowledge of mechanics. Appleton built what they called a roadometer, which could measure the miles accurately.

The leaders soon decided they should leave messages roughly every ten miles for those who came later. One of the messages was left on May 10, enclosed in a box and hung from a twelve-foot pole. With red chalk, they wrote on the box, "Open this and you will find a letter." On the other side they wrote, "Look in this, 316 miles from Winter Quarters. Bound westward. Pioneers." Undoubtedly with a smile on his face, Brigham told Thomas Bullock to write "Platte Post Office" in the upper right hand corner.

The lack of grass for the animals continued as the company rolled farther west. To find more feed, the pioneers sometimes moved away from the Platte River, which caused a new problem: distance from water. They had to depend on wells and creeks. They came to one creek that was nice and clear. But, William

Replica of the pioneers' roadometer.

Clayton wrote, they decided the water could not be used because there were "so many dead buffalo lying in it."

Wells sometimes provided just what they needed. At one camp they found cold water as close as four feet down. One well flowed so much that they could fill a bucket in a minute. All the people and animals had enough to drink.

There was plenty of game on the trail to provide fresh meat, but the hunting became excessive. The needless killing troubled Brigham. Some men shot animals mostly for sport. They took just the best parts for food and left the rest to decay. On May 18, Brigham called together the captains of each group.

"Some members of the company have left meat on the ground and would not use it because it was not a hind quarter," he said. "God has given us a commandment that we should not waste meat, nor take life unless it is needful." He criticized those who "would kill all the game within 100 miles if they could, without one thought of who created it or formed those great pastures for the wild animals to feed in."

"Some men will shoot as much as 30 times at a rabbit if they did not kill it and are continually wasting their ammunition," he declared. "But when they have used all they have got, they may have the pleasure of carrying their empty guns to the mountains."

Wolves and snakes, however, were occasionally dangerous. Like many people in their day, some of the pioneers destroyed these creatures whenever they could. Others avoided killing them if possible.

William Clayton reported meeting up with a rattlesnake one day while he was walking along the river. "It rattled hard," he said. But then it turned and wriggled away without striking. Other men came up and lifted the snake from the track, letting it go free. They decided that if it wasn't necessary to kill it, they shouldn't.

Rattlesnakes were numerous on the prairie, and some were definitely dangerous. Thomas Bullock wrote, "As brother Nathaniel Fairbanks was descending from one of the bluffs, he was bit on the left side of the calf of his left leg, by a very large yellow rattlesnake." The snake escaped into a hole before anyone could kill it.

By the time Nathaniel got back to camp to get medical help, he was suffering from the snake's poison. Thomas wrote that "his tongue was dry, leg swollen, pain in his belly, and eyes dimmer." Luke Johnson treated him with "a corn meal mush poultice" and some medicine. The next day Thomas reported, "This morning Brother Fairbanks was a little easier in pain, but his leg

Rattlesnakes were a common sight along the trail.

was considerably swollen." Nathaniel survived and continued on with the company.

Thomas Bullock narrowly escaped a rattlesnake bite himself. He recorded that he and Luke Johnson were climbing a nearby bluff when "a rattlesnake challenged for battle." The rattling startled Thomas, and he leaped over the snake, calling out to Luke as he did so. Finding Thomas's reaction funny, Luke joked, "If that's the way you fight my friend, I take his part in the battle." When the snake continued to threaten, however, Luke ended up killing it.

On May 20 Thomas recorded, "At ¼ past 10 passed a lone cedar tree having in it the body of an Indian child. It was wrapped in a thin wrapper of straw, then a wrapper of deer skin—also a second deer skin—covered with a buffalo robe, and lashed to the tree with rawhide bands. It had two spoons, a horn and shot pouch attached to it."

The pioneers knew it was an Indian custom to put their dead in trees when available, rather than burying them. After looking over the small corpse, they moved on.

Three days later, on May 23, the travelers passed a formation they called Ancient Ruins Bluff. Several men climbed to the top, carrying a buffalo skull on which they wrote their names.

Replica of a buffalo skull used as a trail marker.

They left it in the southeast corner of the bluff for future travelers to find.

On that day, Harriet recorded, "I am busily engaged baking bread, but my health is poor. Yet I feel that the Lord has blessed me abundantly. I have not had anything of my old disease since I left Winter Quarters. The air is good and seems to brace up our systems that are feeble."

That was on a Sunday. Brigham called a worship meeting in the afternoon. He said some were worrying that it would be too late to plant crops when they got to where they were going. "Well, suppose we did not," he said. "We traveled as fast as our teams were able to go. When we had done all we could, I would feel just as satisfied as if we had 1,000 acres planted in grain." He believed the Lord would help them if they just did the best they could.

Brigham also told the people he was happy "to see so much union and disposition to obey counsel" in the camp. Howard Egan wrote in his journal that it was "a first rate meeting." He said Brigham "gave us some glorious instructions, which done my soul good."

That night there was a high wind, followed by rain and hail. The weather grew very cold. That was not good. They had heard about a company of trappers who traveled in the area when the same thing happened. Sixteen of the trappers' horses had frozen to death in one night.

To keep that from happening, Wilford Woodruff placed blankets on his horses and stayed up most of the night to make sure the animals were all right. They shivered a lot but survived. In the morning, he let them loose to run around and warm themselves up.

That evening, a group of Sioux Indians met up with the camp. "All appeared well armed with muskets," William Clayton noted. He also observed that they were clean and neat. They "were all well dressed," some with "nice robes artfully ornamented with beads and paintings," he wrote.

The Indians had letters to show. The trouble was, they were "written in French and signed by trappers at Fort Laramie," Norton Jacob wrote. The pioneers were able to translate enough of the letters to know that they said the Indians were friendly and would do them no harm.

A Sioux Indian, 1872.

The Saints gave them food and then took them on a tour of the camp. The pioneers pointed out their guns and the cannon. The gunners gave their guests a show, doing mock loadings and firings. William Clayton wrote that this "seemed to please them much."

When it got dark, an elderly Indian leader and his wife indicated they would like to spend the night in the camp. The pioneers obligingly set up a tent and gave them supper. William Clayton wrote, "The old chief amused himself very much by looking at the moon through a telescope for as much as twenty minutes."

The rest of the Indians slept outside the circle of wagons, and the night proved peaceful. After trading some of their items for food and asking for a note of recommendation from the Saints, the Sioux visitors all departed on friendly terms the next morning.

Despite the general good behavior of the pioneers, Brigham grew concerned about what some were doing in their leisure time after several weeks on the trail. When they camped on the night of May 28, Brigham saw several men playing dominoes. That displeased him. Dominoes, like face cards, were sometimes used for gambling. "The devil seems to be getting power over the camp the last several days," Brigham remarked.

President Brigham Young.

Around a campfire that night, he spoke with some of the Church leaders. He talked of the "careless manner" of some of the men and mentioned "levity, loud laughter, whooping and hallooing among the elders." Everybody knew Brigham liked dancing and other amusements as well as anyone else. He said there was no harm in these things if people knew when to stop. But, he said, too much of it led "the mind away from the Lord, and they forgot the object of the journey."

He wanted them all to remember why they were going west. Most people traveling across the plains were in search of land or fortunes. But the Saints in Brigham's company were "pioneers for the whole church of God on the earth, seeking for a place to establish the kingdom."

The next morning was so cold and wet that the pioneers were late getting started. When they were finally ready to go, Brigham called the whole camp together. He had something to say.

The first thing was that he was not going to go with them any farther because of the way they'd been acting. That stunned the company. He said that by now they had left behind those who persecuted them. "We are beyond their reach, we are beyond their power, we are beyond their grasp. What has the devil now to work upon?"

He answered his own question. "Upon the spirits of the men in this camp," he said. "And if you do not open your hearts so that the spirit of God can enter," he prophesied, "you are a ruined people and will be destroyed."

He looked at those gathered around him. "When I wake up in the morning," he said, "the first thing I hear is some of the brethren jawing at each other and quarreling because a horse has got loose in the night. I let the brethren dance and fiddle night after night to see what they will do. But I do not love to see it."

He said some excused their behavior, saying they needed to dance for the exercise. But he said the remedy for that was to walk alongside their wagons and work harder during the day. He scolded them about gambling and playing cards, dominoes, and checkers each evening, while neglecting spiritual matters.

"You don't know how to control your senses," he said. He called upon every man in the camp to "repent of his weakness, of his follies, of his meanness, and every kind of wickedness, and stop your swearing and profane language." He then asked them each to raise a hand to show they would try to repent.

William Clayton recorded, "All

Route followed by the first pioneer company.

covenanted with uplifted hands without a dissenting vote." Some of the other leaders then spoke, all expressing their agreement with what Brigham had preached. This seemed to satisfy him.

The entire company was in a quieter mood when they headed westward again around 1:30 P.M. They traveled about eight miles before heavy rain brought them to an early halt. William Clayton wrote in his journal, "No loud laughter was heard, no swearing, no quarreling, no profane language, no hard speeches to man or beast. It truly seemed as though . . . we had emerged into a new element, a new atmosphere and a new society."

But they still had a long way to go.

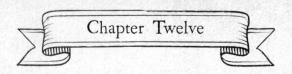

Chapter Twelve

Closer to Zion

By the first of June 1847, the vanguard company of pioneers had been on the trail for about eight weeks. They were tired and hoped to see the Rocky Mountains soon. Somewhere in the valleys beyond those mountains they would find their new home.

Things had improved since Brigham's lecture about changing their ways. The pioneers had developed a general feeling of peace, unity, and brotherly love. Their spirits were lifted further when they reached Fort Laramie in what is now Wyoming and found another group of Latter-day Saints waiting there.

Before Brigham left Nauvoo, he sent men to help gather the Saints in the southern United States. They were to head west from Independence, Missouri, and meet up with the main body of pioneers somewhere along the trail. Fourteen families from Mississippi and other areas followed the Oregon Trail until they arrived near Fort Laramie in 1846. There they learned that Brigham and most of the Saints were still back at Winter Quarters.

Not knowing where Brigham planned to go, the Mississippi

company had turned south to look for a place to wait out the winter. In August they settled at Pueblo in what is now Colorado. The little settlement of Saints grew larger as sick detachments that included men, women, and children arrived from the Mormon Battalion. Some had fallen ill and could not finish the long march with the rest of the volunteer soldiers.

In all, about 275 men, women, and children spent the winter in the Pueblo settlement. In spring 1847, a few of them returned to Fort Laramie to wait for Brigham and his company to arrive. Both groups were excited when they finally came together.

William Clayton wrote, "It caused us much joy to meet with brethren in this wild region and also because we should have some news from the brethren in the army."

Guardhouse at Fort Laramie, Wyoming.

Not all of the news was good. It was sad to hear that some of the men who had marched away in the battalion died from illness or accident. But the sick detachments would soon be getting their pay. Then they and the rest of the Saints from the Mississippi company would go to Fort Laramie to follow the route of the main group.

Church leaders decided to send Amasa Lyman with a few others to meet the Pueblo group. They started out on June 3. Amasa was to carry letters to the battalion members from their families and lead them back to the Mormon Trail. They would then go on to California, where they would receive their final pay and be mustered out of the army. Amasa didn't know it, but the Pueblo Saints were already on the road, headed for Fort Laramie too, hoping to catch up with Brigham.

In the meantime, the Saints already at Fort Laramie joined Brigham's wagon train when it once again headed west on Friday, June 4. The group added three families and a few single men to the pioneer company. William Clayton made a note that one of these

in the evening I visited 'the' entire Camp' and found

Men	Women	Children	Wagons	Horses	Mules	Oxen	Cows	Calves	Bulls	Dogs	Chickens
148	8	5	79	96	51	90	43	9	5	16	16

Thomas Bullock's journal showing his count of the company on June 4, 1847.

men had come as a guide, "knowing the country to the mountains, having traveled it."

William also added that the group had "5 wagons, 1 cart, 11 horses, 24 yoke of oxen, 22 cows, 7 calves," and "3 bulls."

Thomas's final count of the combined company as it left Fort Laramie on June 4 was as follows:

148 men
8 women
5 children
79 wagons
96 horses
51 mules
90 oxen
43 cows
9 calves
3 bulls
16 dogs
16 chickens

On the morning of June 6, 1847, the members of this expanded company were resting on the Sabbath when wagons of Missouri emigrants passed by. Missouri was where the Saints had suffered some of their worst persecutions before they settled in Nauvoo. Missouri governor Lilburn Boggs had issued an order that the Mormons should be exterminated or driven from that state. Despite this history, the two groups on the trail more or less ignored each other.

About an hour later, as some of the Saints were finishing a

prayer meeting, four horsemen approached. They said they were also from Missouri and part of a train of nineteen more wagons coming along the trail. "Some of these are recognized by the brethren, and they seem a little afraid and not fond of our company," William Clayton wrote. "I feel to wish that their fears may follow them even to Oregon."

After the four horsemen departed, the pioneers met together again for a worship service. But when heavy thunder and lightning rolled in with pouring rain, Brigham canceled the service.

During the storm, the nineteen wagons of Missourians came into sight, and Brigham had his men move their cattle out of the way. They watched as the Missourians passed by, led by an Oregon guide. The guide was friendly and told the Saints they could find water in about six miles and after that, no water was available for at least fifteen miles.

The Saints did not normally travel on Sunday. But they knew they could not make the full distance to the second water source in one day. So Brigham ordered the camp to hitch up their teams and move along for five miles.

Along the way, they passed the larger group of Missourians, who had camped in a stand of trees. Several of the Missouri men approached them but not to cause trouble. What the men wanted was to look at the roadometer William Clayton, Orson Pratt, and Appleton Harmon had devised. Someone had told them about the Saints' mileage counter, and they wanted to examine it.

Late that afternoon, Brigham called a halt about halfway

between the two Missouri camps. A man from the larger of the two groups told the Saints his carriage had a broken spring. William Clayton wrote that the man "seemed much troubled to know what to do to get along." The Missourian "asked if there was any man in our company who could fix it." Most wagon trains did not carry such equipment, but the Saints were equipped with three forges. One of the blacksmiths set up his forge and kindly repaired the Missourian's spring.

On June 8 William Clayton recorded an unfortunate incident involving someone from the new Mississippi company members. "About half an hour before we halted," he wrote, "Harriet Crow got run over with one of their wagons. The teams had stopped near the descent from the bluffs, and she stepped on the wagon tongue to get a drink. The cattle started suddenly" and "threw her under the wheel, which passed over her leg below the knee and downwards, passing over her foot above the toes."

Harriet screamed in great pain. "We thought her leg was broken," William wrote, "but were soon satisfied to the contrary. Her foot was badly bruised, but I think there was nothing broken. One of the women washed it

Blacksmith tools.

Harriet Crow was run over by a wagon wheel like one of these.

with camphor. She was then put into a wagon, and we proceeded on."

Traveling together, day in and day out, there were times, as might be imagined, where tempers flared between the pioneers. On June 12, Thomas Bullock recorded that it was a clear, beautiful morning. He had just finished writing in his journal and was getting ready to pack up for the day's travel, when George Brown came to tell him that the cattle needed tending.

Thomas said he would do it, and then he finished his packing. He thought it took him only five or ten minutes, and then he went to take care of the animals and reported back to George.

George, in a huff, asked Thomas why he didn't take care of it right when he said he would, "instead of idling & fooling away your time half an hour."

Thomas was offended and said that was a lie. The men argued back and forth until George hit Thomas with a whip. Thomas cried, "You shall hear of this again, for I shall tell the doctor." He was referring to Willard Richards, who was an herb doctor and an apostle. He belonged to the same group of ten as Thomas and George.

George replied, "You may tell the doctor as soon as you like," and Thomas walked away, ending the incident.

Even though they fought at times, the pioneers also found times to laugh. Lewis Barney, considered a skillful hunter among the pioneers, recorded that he and his hunting partner brought in "more meat than any other two in the camp."

George W. Brown.

Someone gave Porter Rockwell, one of the other hunters, a hard time about that, saying, "What is the matter? You don't kill anything. Here is Barney. He brings in something every day."

"Oh," Porter replied, defending himself, "he kills does and all." Does were female deer. "I could [kill] more than twenty does a day if I would," Porter boasted. "But I don't want to kill old suckling does."

"Better does than nothing," the men said.

Yet Porter said he didn't want anything "but nice fat bucks," or male deer.

The next day Porter came into camp with a skinned antelope and called everyone to come see the "nice buck" he caught. Lewis, thinking Porter's "buck" looked rather small, went to get a closer look. Upon inspection he "found it was an old suckling doe." He called the others to check it out. When the men saw that it was

Orrin Porter Rockwell.

indeed a doe, "they hooted Port for his nice buck."

By mid-June, the Saints had to cross the North Platte River in order to continue west. On Sunday, June 13, they held Sabbath services. After that, Brigham called a meeting with the other leaders to talk about the river crossing.

The river was a problem, being about 100 feet wide and 15 feet deep, with a fast current. The group settled on a plan proposed by Brigham. They would get poles from the mountains and use them to lash wagons together. That would keep them from tipping over as they floated across the river.

But the plan didn't work out very well. "We swam our horses and cattle and crossed our loads in the skiff and at first tried the plan of floating our wagons by extending rope across the river and attaching them," wrote Erastus Snow. "But the current would roll them over as if they were nothing but a log, the wheels and bows appearing alternately upon the surface of the water." They decided that plan was too dangerous.

They tried other ideas that didn't work out well either. Finally, according to Thomas Bullock, Brigham "sent a four-horse team to get timber to make a good raft." When they returned, Brigham combined the new timber with wood already at hand and "went to work with all his strength," aided by others. They made a "first rate" raft that "worked well." Over several backbreaking days, they used the raft to get the wagons onto the other side of the river.

When they started off down the trail again, Brigham asked some of the men to stay at the river crossing with the raft. They were to help other emigrant trains cross the Platte. Then they could join the next company of Saints from Winter Quarters, which were expected to arrive in about a month.

Even before Brigham and his company crossed the river, an emigrant company hired some of the Saints to help them get their belongings across the water. Payment was made in flour at the rate of $2.50 for one hundred pounds. The flour they earned was

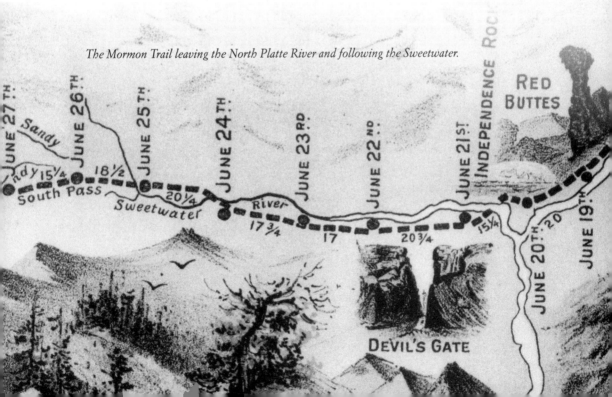

The Mormon Trail leaving the North Platte River and following the Sweetwater.

divided up among the Saints. Each person received five and a half pounds of flour, plus some bacon and meal.

Wilford Woodruff wrote, "It looked as much of a miracle to me to see our flour and meal bags replenished in the midst of the Black Hills as it did to have the children of Israel fed with manna in the wilderness."

On June 19, the Saints left the Platte River behind. They camped that night in a place Wilford Woodruff called "the most wretched of any ground we have found on the way." Though the name of the place was Soda Springs, Brigham suggested it might be called Hell Gate. He said "the water tasted as though it ran through a bed of salt, salts, saltpeter, and sulphur." Heber Kimball said, "It is one of the most humid, swampy, filthy, stinking places imaginable . . . a gloomy, cheerless, filthy place, most dangerous for cattle and unhealthy for families."

That evening they had another encounter with Missourians. Two of the Saints' scouts went to find the next day's camping spot. On the way, they were stopped by six men who wore blankets. As William Clayton wrote, they "had every appearance of being Indians."

The scouts tried to continue on, but the six men motioned for them to go back. When the scouts refused to turn around, the supposed Indians, as William wrote, "put spurs to their horses and were soon out of sight behind a higher piece of land."

The scouts followed them up the ridge. They saw a wagon train of Missourians. The six "Indians" were just entering the camp. The scouts then guessed the supposed Indians were actually Missourians. Very likely they had been trying to drive the Mormons away from a good camping area. When the scouts reported to Brigham, he declared it to be "an old Missouri trick."

On June 21, the pioneers stopped at the Sweetwater River. They were now opposite Independence Rock. Horace Whitney described it as a "lengthy, high mass of rock, somewhat oval in form" that "has quite an isolated appearance, standing, as it does, some distance from the hills by which it is surrounded." During the afternoon rest, several of the pioneers went to examine the rock. They found that earlier travelers had written their names on it.

Wilford Woodruff recorded, "We examined the many names & lists of names of trappers, traders, travelers, and emigrants which are painted upon these rocks. Nearly all the names were put

Independence Rock, in present-day Wyoming.

on with red, black, and yellow paint. Some had washed out and defaced. The greatest number was put on within a few years. Some of them were quite plain of about 30 years standing." Very likely, some of the pioneers added their own names.

On the afternoon of June 23, the Saints finally saw what they had long been looking for. Horace wrote about it, saying, "In advance of us at a great distance can be seen the outlines of mountains, loftier than any we have yet seen. The setting sun throwing its glancing rays athwart their summits reveal them to our eyes covered with snow."

The Rocky Mountains were in sight!

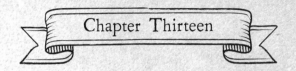

Mountain Fever

Seeing the mountains ahead cheered the exhausted pioneers. That was where they were headed. There they would establish their new homes.

Or would they? They hadn't seen the land yet. Perhaps it would not be suitable after all. Perhaps they would have to search further.

Soon they would know.

On the evening of June 24, 1847, something sad happened. The camp rules called for circling the wagons and putting the horses inside the circle so they would not wander off or be stolen in the night. Suddenly, a young man named John Holman ran into the camp.

"President Young," he hollered. "I have just shot old John."

"John who?" cried Brigham, worried that one of the pioneers was wounded.

The agitated young man answered, "Why, old John, your horse."

Mountain landscape in Utah.

Brigham was somewhat relieved. He had assumed it was a man named John Greene who had been shot.

But old John, his favorite horse? How did it happen?

John Holman, the young man, had been herding the animal into camp. He used his rifle as a prod to move the horse in the right direction. Unfortunately, the gun tangled in the young man's clothing and went off, sending a bullet into the horse's stomach. The horse died later that night.

Brigham mourned the loss of his beautiful, faithful animal. He felt great sorrow, but William Clayton wrote that he "attaches no blame to John who seems grieved very much."

Now that the wagon train was approaching the mountains, the altitude increased and the temperatures dropped. The Saints added layers of clothing to guard against the chilly air. But after the desolation of the prairie, they enjoyed the changed landscape.

"We crossed a small, beautiful creek," recorded Thomas Bullock, and "came to a halt on a beautiful bottom of excellent grass—with plenty of wood, and surrounded by high hills." There they found flowers, wild onions, berry plants, and a mineral spring.

Later on the trail, Thomas said they "ascended a long steep hill, finding many daisies, which was a pleasant sight for me. Brother Wordsworth brought me a ball of snow which I ate; quite a treat for the anniversary of my wedding day." They passed more creeks and flowering strawberry and clover plants. From their view on the trail, they could see three small lakes and a beautiful grove of aspen trees.

But there were drawbacks with the altitude. Although it was warm in the daytime, the air was freezing at night. The quick change in temperatures was blamed for people getting mountain fever. It was not really the cause, though it may have made some people worse. At any rate, several pioneers became miserably ill.

Heber wrote of the sickness, "It affects the eyes, back, and in short the whole system with aches and pains, in most cases accompanied with a sickness at the stomach; it has no appearance of being fatal, and only lasts generally from 1 to 3 days."

June 27 was a Sunday and the anniversary of the mob murder of Joseph and Hyrum Smith at the Carthage jail exactly three years

The Continental Divide near Pacific Springs, Wyoming, early 1900s.

earlier. William Clayton wrote, "It was the general feeling to spend the day in fasting and prayer, but the Gentile companies being close in our rear and feed scarce, it was considered necessary to keep ahead of them."

"Our minds have reverted back to the scenes at Carthage jail," he reflected, "and it is a gratification that we have so far prospered in our endeavors to get from under the grasp of our enemies."

The pioneer company continued on. Later that day, the Saints crossed over the Continental Divide, an imaginary line on the high ridges of the Rocky Mountains. Water on the east side of it flows toward the Atlantic Ocean. On the west side, water flows toward the Pacific Ocean.

At a spot named Pacific Springs, William Clayton wrote, "We

have the satisfaction of seeing the current run west instead of east." And after drinking from a muddy creek, Wilford Woodruff recorded that he "for the first time in my life tasted water running into the Pacific."

While the Saints were at Pacific Springs, they met a company of ten people from Oregon headed east. The Oregonians were transporting furs and skins carried by pack mules. They agreed to carry letters from the pioneers to drop off with the Saints back east.

One of these men was Moses Harris, an experienced mountain man. He had been trapping and exploring in the west for many years. He gave the Saints some issues of a newspaper called the *California Star.* It was published by Samuel Brannan in San Francisco. Sam was a Mormon who had recently led a company of Saints from New York to California. They had traveled on the ship *Brooklyn,* sailing around Cape Horn at the tip of South America.

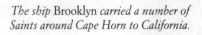

The ship Brooklyn *carried a number of Saints around Cape Horn to California.*

What Moses Harris had to say about the Great Basin, where

Jim Bridger, a mountain man who explored the Great Basin.

the Saints were headed, was discouraging. He said one of the main problems with the area was the lack of timber.

A few days later, the Saints met another well-known mountain man, Jim Bridger. He was headed east on his way to Laramie. The Saints had planned to stop at his fort to talk with him about the Great Basin. He told them that if they would stop and camp right now, he would tell them all about the area.

The Church leaders spent hours with him. He proved to be a talker, going on and on about the Great Basin country and the regions around it. He provided interesting information. Wilford Woodruff commented in his journal, "We found him to have been a great traveler," with "a great knowledge of nearly all Oregon and California . . . if what he told us was true."

Bridger was more positive about the area around the Great Salt Lake than Moses Harris had been. "There was but one thing that could operate against it becoming a great grain country," Wilford Woodruff jotted, and added, "that would be frost." Bridger thought the frost could affect the corn the Saints would try to grow.

The pioneers were somewhat cheered after meeting with

Bridger. They continued on until they reached the Green River and camped on June 30. To their surprise, Sam Brannan himself, along with two companions, appeared at the camp that day. Sam had traveled all the way from San Francisco to tell Brigham that the Saints should go to California.

Samuel Brannan.

Sam had been asked by Brigham to sail with a company of Saints from the eastern United States around Cape Horn. They were to establish a settlement in California. Now Sam tried to convince Brigham that this should be the final destination for all the Saints. He spoke glowingly of the climate and soil there.

But Brigham refused to consider it. Disappointed, Sam and his group soon headed off to Fort Pueblo to find the Saints who remained there. Their intention was to gather up the Mormon Battalion men who had become sick and take some of them to California. There they would be discharged from the army.

Crossing the Green River proved to be a challenge because the water was deep and moving fast. The Saints' experience in building rafts to cross the Platte came in handy. They were able to ferry people and belongings safely over the storm-swollen river. The animals, as usual, swam across on their own.

As the pioneers progressed farther along the trail, more of them developed mountain fever. "Several of the brethren were reported sick, and not able to drive their teams," Howard Egan wrote. "The brethren are all taken alike, with violent pains in the head and back and a very hot fever." It was Orson Pratt's opinion that the sickness was "probably occasioned by suffocating clouds of dust which rise from the sandy road and envelop the whole camp when in motion, and also by the sudden changes of temperature."

Ticks like this one caused mountain fever in many pioneers.

Orson was a scientist, and what he said was what some people thought at the time. They did not know that much of their sickness probably came from getting bitten by ticks. These were tiny spiderlike creatures that lived in the area. They attached themselves to man and beast alike.

Before long the illness spread through the camp. Still, the wagon train rolled on. The company didn't stop to celebrate the Fourth of July. "This is Uncle Sam's day of Independence," Norton Jacob wrote. "Well we are independent of all the powers of the Gentiles, that's enough for us." Other than that, it was a day like any other—hot and dusty, with clouds of mosquitoes.

Wilford Woodruff concluded the day by writing in his journal: "I must stop writing. The mosquitoes have filled my carriage like a cloud and have fallen upon me as though they intend to devour me. I never saw that insect more troublesome than in certain places in this country."

Also on the Fourth, Brigham's brother Phineas and four other volunteers turned around and headed back toward Winter Quarters. They would meet the next company of Saints and guide them along the trail to the valley of the Great Salt Lake. Brigham, Heber, and some of the other men went back with them as far as Green River to help ferry them across.

As they approached the water, they saw a group of men on the other side loading their baggage onto a raft. To their great joy, they discovered it was thirteen men from the Mormon Battalion who had stayed the winter in Pueblo with the Mississippi Saints.

Wilford Woodruff made record of the happy reunion. "When we arrived at the river we saw 13 horsemen on the opposite bank with their baggage on one of our rafts," he wrote. "When we met it was truly a hardy greeting and shaking of hands."

At the river, Brigham said good-bye to his brother Phineas and the others who were going east. Brigham's company and the battalion men then went west again to catch up with the main company.

Thomas Bullock recorded that Brigham and his group arrived at the main camp at 2:15 in the afternoon. They formed a line, and Brigham "spoke a few words." The men from the battalion were

Fort Bridger.

then given "3 cheers for their return," and the group cried out, "Hosanna, Hosanna, Hosanna, Give glory to God and the Lamb."

The pioneer company reached Fort Bridger, in present-day Wyoming, three days later. The fort was a trading post, not a military one. William Clayton wrote in his journal that it was "two double log houses about forty feet long each and joined by a pen for horses about ten feet high constructed by placing poles upright in the ground close together, which is all the appearance of a fort in sight." The pioneers stayed near the fort for two days, shoeing horses and making repairs on their wagons. Some did a bit of trading with the people who lived there.

While at Fort Bridger, Wilford Woodruff went to a nearby brook to try his hand at fly fishing. With a fishing pole he had brought from England, he fixed his "reel, line, and artificial fly." The men at the fort told him there weren't many trout in the stream, and some of the pioneers were already fishing there with meat and grasshoppers, "but," Wilford wrote, "no one seemed to catch any."

Wilford flung his artificial fly out onto the brook's surface and watched it carefully. Soon, he wrote, "I saw the nimble trout dart my fly, hook himself, and run away with the line. But I soon worried him out and drew him to shore." Wilford caught twelve fish that day.

After the Saints left Fort Bridger, they faced what William Clayton called "the most mountainous course we have yet seen." To make

Wagon ruts on the Mormon Trail.

matters worse, a number of men were so sick they couldn't drive their wagons without the help of others.

A big problem now was the steepness of the mountains they were climbing. "Almost perpendicular," Thomas Bullock wrote about the trail. He commented that "looking back from the bottom looks like jumping off the roof of a house to a middle story, then from the middle story to the ground." He thanked God that he didn't have an accident on that stretch.

Brigham and Heber warned everyone to be careful. "They locked the wheels of some wagons themselves," Thomas recorded. This was their way of applying brakes, and it kept the wagons from plunging downhill.

Brigham had been setting the pace ever since they left Winter Quarters. He worked at any job he felt needed him. But on July 12, as the pioneers were nearing their final destination, he too became ill with the mountain fever. He was so sick that he remained behind as the group moved on. He suffered from terrible headaches and fever. The joints in his body ached. He later described himself as "almost mad with pain."

After all his hard work and wise leadership, he was not going to be one of the first to see the valley that he hoped would be their new home.

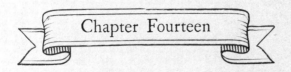

Chapter Fourteen

This Is the Place

Brigham was so ill that he could not travel for three days. A few men remained behind with him when the rest of the wagon train moved on. His companions did what they could to make him comfortable. At midday on July 15, 1847, he was still sick but well enough to catch up to the main camp.

A group of twenty-three wagons with forty-two men had been sent ahead with Orson Pratt to find the best route over the mountains. The trail was barely passable. Several men with shovels and axes had to clear the way before the wagons could follow.

By the evening of July 16, the main group had traveled over sixteen miles to where, as William Clayton wrote, "we are yet enclosed by high mountains on each side." Wilford Woodruff wrote that they "had a bad road for the sick to travel." Brigham was so ill the next day that after traveling just three miles, he could not go on. In fact, it was rumored through the camp that he was "nigh unto death."

Since they had found a spot with good water and plenty of

The Needles, along the trail in present-day Wyoming.

feed for the animals, the entire train stopped for the day. While Brigham rested, some of the men went to the privacy of a grove to pray for him and the other sick members in camp. During the course of the day, they fished in a nearby stream or, as Thomas Bullock recorded, "amused themselves by rolling large rocks down the hills."

The next day was the Sabbath, and they did not travel. Brigham was still not feeling well on Monday. Several men volunteered to stay behind and care for him in a slower-moving group. He was improving but still slowly. The rest of the company carried on at a normal pace.

Brigham continued to travel in a bed made up for him in Wilford Woodruff's carriage, which was not as bouncy as a wagon. Even so, after traveling over what Wilford described as "the worst road we have had on the journey," Brigham was "quite weary come night."

In the meantime, the advance company, led by Orson Pratt, was progressing with the trail making. On July 20, Orson wrote out a detailed letter about the area they were heading toward. He left it for the people in the rest of the group to find when they came by.

The valley of the Great Salt Lake lay just ahead. On July 21, Orson Pratt and Erastus Snow rode out ahead of the others in the advance company to scout the trail. Climbing a hill at the mouth of the canyon, they suddenly found themselves with a marvelous view.

Orson wrote, "A broad open valley about 20 miles wide and 30 long lay stretched out before us, at the north end of which the broad waters of the Great Salt Lake glistened in the sunbeams, containing high mountainous islands from 25 to 30 miles in extent." After being in the mountains for so long and suddenly seeing the valley, he wrote, "We could not refrain from a shout of joy which almost involuntarily escaped from our lips the moment this grand and lovely scenery was within our view."

Having reached the Salt Lake Valley, the two men spent some time exploring it. Then they returned back up the canyon to join others in the advance company.

First glimpse of the Salt Lake Valley by the advance party.

That evening, Orson received a letter from Willard Richards and George A. Smith, who were in the group behind. They said they found the message Orson had written for them on the trail. "We left Brother Young day before yesterday," the letter said. "His health was improving, but he was not able to travel as fast as the camp." The letter indicated that they weren't too far away and concluded, "We expect they are coming leisurely on."

The letter contained Brigham's instructions about the valley based on information he had learned earlier, and it mentioned some of the Indians who lived nearby at a place called Utah Lake. Brigham "felt inclined for the present not to crowd upon the Utes until we have a chance to get acquainted with them." He wrote that "it would be better to bear toward the region of the Salt Lake, rather than the Utah Lake and find some good place for our seeds and deposit them as speedily as possible, regardless of a future location."

The letter went on to say that they should proceed as they had been doing "until you arrive at some point in the Basin, where you could 'hear' the potatoes grow, if they had only happened to have been there." At that point, Brigham instructed, "Let all your mechanics, even to the rough hewers, be employed in fitting up plows, while all your horses and mules should be employed in small companies in scouring the country in every direction."

"By night," Brigham said, "you will be able to get a tolerable good report from the various companies and begin to judge where

Wagons traveling through Echo Canyon in what is now Utah.

will be the best spot to put in the plows." Brigham and his group were still behind, but, he said, "we hope to be there to hear the report, as we anticipate we will not be more than one day behind you; and we expect the whole camp will be on hand in a day or two following."

Since it was urgent to start growing food, the letter instructed, "The time for planting is fully come, and we feel anxious to make every move that would facilitate the potato crop; it matters not where it is."

The main camp of Saints had been struggling to follow the rough trail traced by Orson and his group. On July 22, they saw what they had been looking for. Thomas Bullock wrote that they viewed "the Salt Lake in the distance with its bold hills on its islands towering up in bold relief behind the silvery lake." He expressed his happiness, saying, "I could not help shouting 'hurra, hurra, hurra, there's my home at last.'"

Thomas described the scene with enthusiasm: "The sky is very clear, the air delightful and altogether looks glorious; the only drawback appearing to be the absence of timber." But he was not discouraged, for, he wrote, "there is an ocean of stone in the mountains to build stone houses and walls for fencing. If we can only find a bed of

A plow like those used by the pioneers to break ground for planting crops.

View of the Salt Lake Valley.

coal, we can do well and be hidden up in the mountains unto the Lord."

The members of the main camp descended from their high viewing point to a lower level, where they camped for the night. Early the next morning, they packed up and traveled the two miles to where they intended to start farming. As soon as they arrived, Thomas recorded that Orson Pratt called them together to offer up a "prayer to Almighty God, returning thanks for the preservation of the camp, their prosperity in the journey, and safe arrival in this place."

The members of the camp put together their plows, as Brigham had instructed, and started plowing. The first furrow was dug at noon. For the next few days they worked four-hour shifts until the potatoes, corn, beans, and buckwheat were planted. They appointed committees to oversee locating places for planting, to prepare tools, to tend the animals, and to make a coal pit.

Brigham still hadn't yet seen the valley at this point. He was very weak from his bout with the mountain fever. But he finally reached a high pass where he could see a long distance.

On July 23, his history records, "I ascended and crossed over the Big Mountain, when on its summit I directed Elder Woodruff, who had kindly tendered me the use of his carriage, to turn the same half way round so that I could have a view of a portion of Salt Lake Valley. The spirit of light rested upon me and hovered over the valley, and I felt that there the Saints would find protection and safety. We descended and encamped at the foot of the Little Mountain."

Not everyone was enthusiastic about their new home, however. Harriet Young, Lorenzo's wife, had been unhappy about the lack of trees for much of the journey. Now they had arrived at a place that to her seemed a wasteland. It seemed barren and dry with few trees.

Gazing out at the scene before her, feeling tired and ill, she wrote, "This day we arrived in the valley of the great Salt Lake. My feelings were such as I cannot describe. Everything looked gloomy, and I felt heartsick." Even though she had traveled a great

Brigham Young views the Salt Lake Valley for the first time.

distance to reach that point, she wrote that she would "willingly travel a thousand miles farther" to reach a better place to live.

Fortunately, there were not many who shared that opinion. Harriet's daughter Clara had been miserable at the beginning of the long trek. She later shared that "she never felt so badly in her life as when she was actually starting on this uncertain pilgrimage." That was because she thought "they didn't know where they were going; only that it was across the plains."

The idea of leaving the society of the Church members "seemed dreadful to her." But she remained positive, believing "all would be right." And "when they had really reached their destination she was relieved, and really satisfied. It didn't look so dreary to her as to the other ladies."

On July 24, Brigham Young and Wilford Woodruff finally emerged from the last canyon. Wilford expressed their feelings when he wrote, "We came in full view of the great valley or basin" of "the Salt Lake and land of promise, held in reserve by the hand of God for a resting place for the Saints."

Brigham and Wilford admired the length and breadth of the Salt Lake Valley. Wilford commented on the heavy vegetation, the large lake with its islands, and the streams and rivers that flowed from the mountains toward it. He thought about the "hard journey from Winter Quarters," a trip of more than a thousand miles. After all that—after all the pain and strain and sickness—they were finally at their destination.

"Our hearts were surely made glad," Wilford wrote.

Wilford recorded how they looked out on the beautiful valley, with its surrounding mountains, and pictured the day that "the House of God" would rise and "the standard be unfurled for the nations to gather there."

"President Young expressed his full satisfaction in the appearance of the valley as a resting place for the Saints," Wilford wrote.

From the mouth of the canyon, Brigham and his small band pressed forward, joining the larger groups that already had gone ahead into the valley. July 24 went down in history as the day that Brigham Young and those traveling with him entered the Salt Lake Valley, the new home for the Saints.

Later, the feelings Brigham expressed as he looked out upon the valley that day would be reduced to four simple, easy to remember words: "This is the place."

Afterword

Eventually, other Saints who were scattered across the plains arrived to join those first pioneers. After just a month in the valley, Brigham Young returned to Winter Quarters. Later that year, at a conference in Kanesville, Iowa, on the east side of the Missouri River, he was sustained as president of The Church of Jesus Christ of Latter-day Saints.

View of the Salt Lake Valley from the north, 1853.

The next year, 1848, Brigham led another company of Saints to the Salt Lake Valley. It was the last time he ever crossed the plains.

Under his direction, Salt Lake City became the headquarters of the Church. Tens of thousands more pioneers gathered there in the decades that followed. These pioneers helped build a house of God, a temple, just as Brigham had foreseen.

They would be astounded if they could see the valley today with its large business districts and numerous neighborhoods. Worldwide, there are many millions of members of The Church of Jesus Christ of Latter-day Saints. And nearly every year, beginning in 1849, the Saints have celebrated July 24 to remember the remarkable story of Brigham Young and the first pioneers.

The Salt Lake Temple under construction, 1883.

The completed Salt Lake Temple, 1896.

Recommended Reading

In writing this book, the authors relied on many primary and secondary sources. Most of the primary sources are easily accessible in the database titled "Mormon Pioneer Overland Travel, 1847–1868," found at history.lds .org/overlandtravels. The principal secondary sources are as follows:

Arrington, Leonard J. *Brigham Young: American Moses.* New York: Alfred A. Knopf, 1985.

Bennett, Richard E. *We'll Find the Place: The Mormon Exodus, 1846–1848.* Salt Lake City: Deseret Book, 1997.

Knight, Hal, and Stanley Kimball. *111 Days to Zion.* Salt Lake City: Big Moon Traders, 1997.

Leonard, Glen M. *Nauvoo: A Place of Peace, a People of Promise.* Salt Lake City: Deseret Book; Provo, Utah: Brigham Young University Press, 2002.

Turner, John G. *Brigham Young: Pioneer Prophet.* Cambridge, Mass.: Belknap Press of Harvard University Press, 2012.

Readers who want additional information are encouraged to turn to these sources, especially the original records of the pioneers found in the database.

Image Credits

Images are used courtesy The Church of Jesus Christ of Latter-day Saints, Church History Library, and are in public domain unless noted otherwise below. All images are used by permission.

Page i, 6, 82, 89, 108, 119: Details, lithograph of the Mormon Trail.

Page 2: *Massacre of Mormons at Haun's Mill*, engraving in Charles Mackay, *History of the Mormons, or Latter-day Saints* (ca. 1851).

Page 3: *Joseph Mustering the Nauvoo Legion*, by C. C. A. Christensen, courtesy Brigham Young University.

Page 4: *Carthage Jail*, by Frederick Piercy.

Page 5: *Brigham Young*, by Frederick Piercy.

Page 11: Detail, "Bill of Particulars," *Nauvoo Neighbor*, Oct. 29, 1845.

Page 12: Compass, musket, and kettle, courtesy LDS Church History Museum.

Page 13: Ox, © Morphart Creation/ shutterstock.com.

Page 14: Daguerreotype of Nauvoo Temple, ca. 1847.

Page 18: Mississippi River, © Jorg Hackemann/ shutterstock.com.

Page 20: Howard Roscoe Driggs Church Historic Sites Tour, 1909.

Page 23: *Migration from Nauvoo*, by Charles B. Hall.

Page 24: *Nauvoo*, by Frederick Piercy.

Page 25: *Nauvoo Temple Ruins*, by Frederick Piercy.

Page 26: *Exodus from Nauvoo*, by C. C. A. Christensen.

Page 32: *Sugar Creek*, by C. C. A. Christensen.

Page 33: Pioneer shoe, © TracieGrant/ shutterstock.com

Page 35: Bread, © Valentyn Volkov/ shutterstock.com.

Page 37: Garden Grove Cemetery, by George Lofstrom Strebel, ca. 1936.

Page 38: *Council Bluffs Ferry*, by Charles B. Hall.

Page 40: Engraving, Hubert Howe Bancroft, *History of Utah* (1890).

Page 41: *Battalion Ball*, by C. C. A. Christensen; engraved portrait of Thomas L. Kane in Orson F. Whitney, *History of Utah* (1904).

Page 43: *Enlistment of Mormon Battalion at Winter Quarters*, by Charles B. Hancock.

Page 44: *Scene of Battalion Boys in California*, by Charles B. Hancock.

Page 46: Detail, *Warsaw Signal*, 1846.

Page 49: *Mob Burning Morley's Settlement*, by C. C. A. Christensen.

Page 51: Detail, *Hancock Eagle*, July 13, 1846.

Page 56: *Expulsion of Saints from Nauvoo*, by Charles B. Hancock.

Page 59: *Camp at Keokuk*, by Frederick Piercy.

Page 61: *Miracle of the Quails*, by C. C. A. Christensen.

Page 62: Quail, © Janet Mary Kruckenberg.

Page 64: *Entrance to Kanesville, or Council Bluffs*, by Charles B. Hall.

Page 65: Mill at Winter Quarters, by George Lofstrom Strebel, 1936.

Page 66: Detail, Patty Sessions's journal, 1846.

Page 69: Mount Pisgah marker on the Mormon Trail, by George Lofstrom Strebel, 1936.

Page 70: Engraving by Charles B. Hall.

Page 71: Mary Haskin Parker Richards, ca. 1850s.

Page 73: Gristmill in City Creek Canyon, Salt Lake City, Utah, ca. late 1800s.

Page 74: Log cabin in Salem, Illinois, by Don Enders.

Page 76: Detail, roll of pioneer company 1, 1847.

Page 79: Wagon train in Echo Canyon, Charles W. Carter Glass Negative Collection, 1867.

Page 81: Engraving of John Taylor by Charles B. Hall; portrait of Parley P. Pratt by Edward Martin.

Page 86: Bugle, © Gavran333/shutterstock.com.

Page 92: American bison, © David Osborn/shutterstock.com.

Page 94: Detail, Horace Whitney journal, 1847.

Page 95: *Buffalo at Scotts Bluff*, by Charles B. Hall.

Page 96: Buffalo bones, © Momo5287/shutterstock.com.

Page 98: *Burning a Refuge to Escape from the Oncoming Prairie Fire*, by Frederic Remington, ca. 1907, courtesy Library of Congress.

Page 102: Rattlesnake, © Hein Nouwens/shutterstock.com.

Page 103: Replica of a buffalo skull, courtesy LDS Church History Museum.

Page 105: Good Hawk-Ha-V-Ka-Washta. Chawana Sioux, ca. 1872, courtesy U.S. National Archives.

Page 111: Guardhouse at Fort Laramie, Wyoming, by George Lofstrom Strebel, ca. 1936.

Page 115: Blacksmith tools, © FotograFFF/shutterstock.com.

Page 116: Detail, wagons in Echo Canyon, Utah, Charles W. Carter Glass Negative Collection, ca. 1867.

Page 121: Independence Rock, Wyoming, ca. 1900.

Page 122: Mountain clearing, © Earl D. Walker/shutterstock.com.

Page 124: Charles W. Carter Glass Negative Collection, ca. 1870s.

Page 126: Continental Divide, by Andrew Jenson.

Page 127: *Brooklyn*, by Duncan McFarlane.

Page 128: Jim Bridger, Charles W. Carter Glass Negative Collection, ca. 1870s.

Page 130: Tick, © Hein Nouwens/shutterstock.com.

Page 132: *Fort Bridger*, by M. D. Houghton.

Page 133: Wagon ruts on the Mormon Trail, by George Lofstrom Strebel, ca. 1936.

Page 136: The Needles, Wyoming, Charles W. Carter Glass Negative Collection, ca. 1870s.

Page 138: *First Glimpse of "The Valley,"* by Charles B. Hall.

Page 139: Wagon train in Echo Canyon, Utah, Charles W. Carter Glass Negative Collection, ca. 1870s.

Page 140: Plow, © arogant/shutterstock.com.

Page 141: *Great Salt Lake Valley*, by Charles B. Hall.

Page 143: Illustration, Hubert Howe Bancroft, *History of Utah* (1890).

Page 145: *Great Salt Lake City*, by Frederick Piercy.

Border on pages i–iii: © DmitryPrudnichenko/shutterstock.com.

Frames on pages 5, 71, 81, 84: © Iakov Filimonov/shutterstock.com.

Frame on page 14: © Lynn2511/shutterstock.com.

Frame on page 106: © Vronska/shutterstock.com.

Frame on page 127: © Kittibowornphatnon/shutterstock.com.

Background: © ilolab/shutterstock.com.

Endsheets: Lithograph of the Mormon Trail.